Gyles Brandreth is a former Oxford Scholar, President of the Oxford Union, Artistic Director of the Oxford Theatre Festival, founder of the British Pantomime Association, Organiser of the National Scrabble Championships, European Monopoly Champion and holder of the world record for the longest-ever after-dinner speech – eleven hours! He has written for a dozen national newspapers and magazines and his weekly Alphabet Soup column is syndicated throughout the United States. He has made over a thousand appearances on radio and TV in the UK, the USA and Australia and sold more than six million copies of his many books.

Also by Gyles Brandreth in Futura paperback

THE BOOK OF MISTAIKES
THE SCRABBLE PUZZLE BOOK

GYLES BRANDRETH

The Book of Excuses

Futura
Macdonald & Co
London & Sydney

A Futura Book

ISBN 0 7088 2452 8

Typeset, printed and bound in Great Britain by
Hazell Watson & Viney Limited,
Member of the BPCC Group,
Aylesbury, Bucks

Futura Publications
A Division of
Macdonald & Co (Publishers) Ltd
Maxwell House
74 Worship Street
London EC2A 2EN
A BPCC plc Company

CONTENTS

ANY EXCUSE IS BETTER THAN NONE

Who needs an excuse? We all do. At least, that's my excuse for writing this book. It is intended as a helpful handbook for those who don't have an excuse – and need one. In the pages that follow you will find excuses of every kind, from *famous excuses* ('I lost the fight because I've been slimming too fast' – Muhammad Ali) to *infamous* ones ('I can't marry you Deirdre. A Mormon's only allowed six wives and I've got half-a-dozen already.')

The sort of excuse you settle on depends very much on the circumstances. You might choose to stick your neck out and go for the *bold excuse*:

> One wheel went into a ditch, my feet jumped from the brake to the accelerator, I leapt across to the other side of the road and jumped into the trunk of a tree.

If you have a sudden brainwave, go for the *inspired excuse* like the Middlesbrough man who was brought before Teeside Crown Court in May 1973 for showing contempt by raising two fingers to a High Court judge. He was released after explaining that he mistook His Lordship for the local mayor.

Then there are those euphemistic excuses so beloved of local authorities, government spokesmen and most commercial organizations – phrases like: 'Under active consideration', which means 'We're searching the files for it'; 'The matter is currently being surveyed,' which means 'We need more time to come up with an answer'; and 'for the enthusiast' which, when applied to cars, suggests that

7

the previous owners have spent more time underneath than in the driving seat.

Official excuses come in other forms too. There was a district council anxious to make savings and be seen to do so. The council decided not to spend anything on its roads in the year in question because it realized there wouldn't be any money left in the kitty after paying the expenses of members attending the meetings.

Town Halls and government departments also lead the field when it comes to *optimistic excuses*. Take the case of one official spokesman who excused the fact that Britain had been left behind in the space race on the grounds that we lead the world in sewage treatment . . .

Parents also have a knack of looking on the bright side when they resort to the *protective excuse*. After her son's bout of high jinks made headlines in a local paper a Birmingham mother said:

> I was with Ian while he was at the Club. He is not uncontrollable. He is big, but then boys are bigger than girls. None of the other mothers complained to me. Ian did shut Mrs Carter's little girl in a trunk. He's a naturally tidy child and puts all his things away.

In this book you will find excuses for all occasions. From talking your way out of a speeding fine to talking your way out of bed. And from explaining your lack of form on the field to explaining why you are late for work – there are excuses to suit every situation and every need.

As someone who's spent a lifetime concocting excuses, I should know!

BEST OF·BRITISH

As a breed we British tend to excuse ourselves either by blaming others, or by taking up a stand that's so illogical it's disarming . . .

This is a letter from a rainwear retailer to a dissatisfied customer:

> Dear Madam,
> With reference to your blue raincoat, our manufacturers have given the garment in question a thorough testing, and find that it is absolutely waterproof. If you will wear it on a dry day, and then take it off and examine it, you will see that our statement is correct.

☆

From a statement by the Chairman of the Beecham Group in his Annual Report:

> Naturally enough for a company the size of Beecham, the year brought its problems. The pharmaceutical side of the business, including proprietary medicines, was clearly not helped by the very low level of winter sickness throughout the northern hemisphere.

☆

Such has been the pressure on British designers in the past that many major developments have been 'approved' without adequate testing. Witness the sad fate of a prototype muck-spreader that passed straight from the drawing-board to the workshop, the intermediary checks having been sidestepped with a summary 'No time, issue the drawings and get on with the next part of the job'. Come the day of the test-run a group of would-be customers and design staff gathered to see the first full load sent on its way. This was not a happy day for British agriculture. About the only area that remained uncovered by the hail of manure was that designated as the target. The spectators and the wretched operator were liberally showered by a deluge of effluent powerful both in velocity and odour.

As a spokesman explained afterwards, 'There were quite a number of places in the gear train where a left-hand helix angle instead of a right-handed one would have made a deal of difference to the success of the demonstration.'

From the accounts department of a large department store:

Dear Sir/Madam,
You have been served with your cactus by our Rainwear Staff. We have unfortunately been unable to teach our computer the difference between an umbrella and a cactus. Therefore, on your next monthly statement, your cactus will be described as an umbrella.

☆

The Ford Motor Company once carried out an investigation into the causes of crashes involving their cars. One of the results was the interesting statistic that ten per cent of the accidents involved collisions with lamp-posts, which led to the logical conclusion by one company researcher that 'the country's lamp-posts generally are badly positioned'.

☆

Footwear, we might imagine, is designed to make it more comfortable for us when we walk from A to B. When one irate customer returned a very costly pair of shoes to an exclusive West End boutique after they had fallen apart in the course of only three wearings, she was told, 'I am sorry, madam, we do not cater for pedestrians.'

☆

Sign in a shop in Sunbury:

In order to maintain a high standard of service to our customers, this branch will be closed all day on Thursdays.

☆

Broken eggs are a major headache to the poultry industry. In spite of measures taken to minimize these losses, the bill still runs into millions of pounds each year. Asked to account for this continuing wastage, one leading researcher explained that some hens stand on tiptoe to lay, with the result that their eggs land harder on the ground.

☆

A correspondent in the AA magazine *Drive* once had occasion to write, 'Within a month I had to have a new petrol tank fitted, the windscreen motor burnt out, the water pump developed a leak, the clock didn't work. But you expect teething troubles.'

☆

Forty years ago the idea of holding Sunday choral classes in another village school was turned down when one of the village elders objected that it was 'the first step towards a Continental Sunday'.

☆

A Cambridgeshire housewife bought more than she bargained for when she settled on an ice cream gateau for the family tea. As she explained to the manufacturers, there was nothing wrong with the gateau itself. What alarmed her was the word SEX written across the top in large white letters. Full of apologies the manufacturers replaced the gateau without question and wrote back explaining that the message had been a parting shot from a worker who had just been dismissed.

☆

From a company circular:

Dear Customer,
The British firm Digitronics Ltd. has changed its name to Digitronix Ltd., to avoid confusion with a US firm with a similar sounding name.

CLOCKING IN

You're late. Those expecting you know you're late. They're livid. What do you say? 'Punctuality,' said Oscar Wilde, 'is the thief of time,' but assuming that inspiration like this escapes you, here are a few suggestions.

Oversleeping excuses

We put the clocks back a week too early.

The dog pulled out the plug of the clock-radio.

One of our neighbours is building a cabin cruiser. His power-saw and drill keep us awake until two every morning.

I've been using a telephone service to wake me for the last two weeks. It was working fine until this morning, when their switchboard went on the blink.

The thermostat in the electric blanket has gone haywire and roasted us all night. We didn't get to sleep until four when we finally ripped it out of the bed.

I went to a concert last night and I couldn't hear the alarm. What did you say? Speak up!

I got in from the airport late and exhausted. I must have set the alarm on New York time.

Late home from the office excuses

The line was engaged when I rang to say I'd been called to an emergency meeting.

You know it's a new car and has to be driven gently. I shouldn't go above thirty-five for the first 1,000 miles.

I saw something in a sale that suited you down to the ground, but by the time I got there, it had gone. They suggested their other branch but that was closed when I arrived.

One of the chaps in Export has just been deserted by his wife. He wanted someone to talk to so I had to take him for a drink to keep an eye on him. We're worried he's hitting the bottle.

I just nipped up a few floors before leaving when the lift overshot and deposited me two floors too high. I thought I'd better walk down. Then I discovered the doors all had one-way locks and I couldn't get anyone to open the one on the tenth. I had to walk all the way to the ground-floor and even then it took a quarter of an hour to get the security man to let me out. By that stage the office was locked and when I finally made it to the station the train had gone.

We were having such a good game that when I noticed a free court forty-five minutes later I couldn't resist taking it. You know how it is.

Rendez-vous excuses

You were waiting outside Harrods? But you definitely said 'See you in Selfridges.' That's where I've been for the last hour, listening to the stereos and trying on track suits.

I know it should have been yesterday. I've only just realized I've been going by last year's calendar.

But I was there. Where on earth were you?

You were in a hurry, but believe me you said seven o'clock not six. As it was, I was there at six but, knowing I was an hour early, I popped into the pub to kill time.

The bus broke down in the middle of nowhere and we had to wait for a relief. I started walking but couldn't get a lift until the replacement bus passed me an hour and a half later. They made me pay twice!

You might have made it clear which Upper Richmond Road you meant. I've been chasing around for thirty-five minutes trying to avoid a snooping traffic warden.

I bought you some flowers but some idiot barged into me and they got crushed all over my shirt and suit. I had to go back and change, and there's no way of phoning you here.

DRINKS ON THE HOUSE

There are two types of drinking excuse. One for having a drink. One for having had too many. There's no need for an excuse for anything in between.

A defendant at Bradford City Court a couple of years ago pleaded guilty to being drunk and disorderly. He explained, 'I have been having treatment for my drinking and I had a drink to see if they'd cured me.'

☆

Notice in a village hall in 1935:

The population will then adjourn to the village hall to drink the health of the King in ale. Port wine will be supplied to those who are teetotallers, in accordance with an old British custom.

☆

In a recent court appearance the defendant, a proud father, was charged with being drunk in charge of a pram. 'Wine makes me happy,' he told the court. 'I was pretending to be drunk to entertain my child.'

☆

One of Leeds' more disreputable senior citizens, Mr Geoffrey Lawson, made a memorable court appearance in May 1971 charged for the 500th time with drunkenness. The court was told that the charge was first brought against him 49 years earlier, in 1922, and he was given an absolute discharge. A bare two days later he appeared in front of the bench once more; on his 501st charge he told

16

the magistrates, 'I was celebrating my anniversary.' This time the magistrates fined him 50p.

From the *Kent Messenger*:

> The magistrates queried an application for an occasional licence to sell intoxicating liquor at the first anniversary celebrations of the Sheerness Temperance Club.

Charles Dearden, described as an aircraft fitter of the Duke of York public house, was fined £100 at Taunton Crown Court after being found guilty of driving a three-wheeler while under the influence of alcohol. In his defence he said that he was an amateur fire-eater and had swallowed turpentine and paraffin prior to his breath-test in connection with a fire-swallowing performance.

☆

'That's the twelfth time you've been to the bar,' a wife reproached her husband at the annual company binge. 'What will people think?'
'It's all right,' he replied. 'I tell everybody I'm getting something for you.'

☆

A man who'd spent the previous night with a business colleague was taken to task by his wife the following morning. 'When you came home you told me you'd been to the Grand Hotel with that Mr Evans. I've just been chatting with his wife and she says you were both at the Trocadero. Why didn't you tell me the truth?'
'When I got in last night I couldn't say "Trocadero",' her husband admitted.

17

How many friends would we have left if I gave up?

Don't you know that we're supposed to be saving water?

Now that we make our own we can afford a little fun.

Any doctor will tell you that a little wine is good for the stomach.

You know I don't really enjoy it, but it's part of the business. No lunchtime drinks – no contract.

If God had wanted us to stay on the wagon he wouldn't have created fermentation.

There's a report recently published that shows that people who drink live longer than those who don't. (This may sound too good to be true but somewhere there's a report 'recently published' that'll prove just about anything.)

Dr Johnson once drank thirty glasses of port at one sitting and it never did him any harm.

It helps me unwind.

It's a sign of virility.

I've learned the secret. Drink a litre of water before bed and there's no hangover in the morning.

I never mix drinks and I never suffer.

Why collect miniatures? Everyone does that. With full-size bottles you're in another league.

Would you prefer people to think we couldn't afford it?

I'm always more fun when I've had a few.

The alternative's still illegal and I never break the law.

I only do it to keep my husband/wife company.

Compared with what I used to put away this is nothing.

An appreciation of good wine is the best insurance against old age. Even when you can't walk to the supermarket and when your sight and hearing aren't what they used to be, you've still got a cultivated palate.

I've been drinking for long enough to know how much I can take.

EVENING, OFFICER

When it comes to excuses, just ask a policeman; he's heard them all before – and he's made one or two in his time.

When George Oldfield, then Assistant Chief Constable of West Yorkshire, was asked if he'd be looking to Scotland Yard to help in tracking down the murderer masquerading as Jack the Ripper, he replied, 'Why should I? They haven't caught theirs yet.'

A man apprehended early one morning by Croydon police in business premises that did not belong to him, was asked why he was carrying a heavy iron gate hinge. He was about to make a birdcage, he told them.

A man caught red-handed with a half-dozen frozen chickens stolen from a supermarket was adamant that he'd only taken them to throw at his wife.

A cyclist fined £2 for riding in a dangerous manner was asked why he had been riding with both hands off the handlebars holding up a magazine. 'It's the only chance I get of reading,' he explained.

A contingent of police sent to supervise a National Front meeting in Brixton contained one officer blessed with unusual foresight. Asked the time by one of the crowd, he replied that he'd left his watch at home in case it got damaged in any violence.

☆

A Capuchin friar was caught by Italian customs officers trying to smuggle cigarettes across the border. He put up a convincing performance when confronted with the evidence, by maintaining that he thought he was carrying macaroni. He would have 'thrown it into the lake with my own hands', he told the police, had he realized his error.

☆

In 1972 a French medical student at the University of Marseilles shot dead one of the teaching staff. Asked to explain his action, he told the police that the tutor had been a hindrance to his medical career.

☆

The disappearance of a large number of sparking plugs from a Denver factory led police to the home of one of the firm's employees. Inside they found a hoard of 290,000 plugs. 'I just like to see them around,' was the thief's explanation.

☆

An unemployed labourer found in a Kent bank well after closing time was asked by police exactly what he was up to. 'I've come about my overdraft,' he told them.

☆

Resentment which mounted over thirty years brought a dramatic end to the friendship of two old dining partners. Every night John Quartero and Joe Cocito sat down to supper together and every night they devoured apparently the same fare – ravioli, which Joe prepared with loving care. Unfortunately, John found Joe's seasoning too powerful. At first this was only a mild irritation but over the thirty years the sauce got hotter and John's patience subjected to increasing strain. In the end he couldn't stand the tension any longer and stormed out in the middle of one meal without saying a word to Joe. The next day he shot him in the leg. The police charged him with assaulting Joe with a deadly weapon and, full of remorse, John told them, 'I couldn't stand Joe's hot sauce any longer.'

☆

Detectives investigating a case of attempted murder were told by their suspect, 'I was repairing his car and accidentally hit him on the head. Somehow it developed and I put my arms round his neck and strangled him. Have you ever had one of those days when nothing goes right?'

☆

Passers-by raised more than a few eyebrows at the antics of a girl in Euston Road, London, when they saw her calmly stripping off her clothes and proceeding along the pavement stark naked. The girl, who soon found herself being whisked away in a police car, blamed a four-letter word on a nearby building site for her action. As someone used to doing 'what comes naturally', when she saw the word 'shed' written on a sign, she obeyed the instruction.

☆

Croydon police were amused to discover a visiting American musician lurking in a shop doorway at 3.30 one morning equipped with a hammer, a screwdriver and a spanner. They were even more amused when he told them, 'I was just going to make a guitar.'

☆

The Scottish tradition of first-footing took on a special meaning one Hogmanay for a Scotsman living in the Isle of Wight. Returning home in the early hours of 1 January, Mr Gordon Lunn stumbled across a break-in, or so he claimed.

'I heard a crash of glass from the shop,' he later told the police. 'I saw two men running and spotted what I thought was another man in the window. I crawled through the hole in the glass and leapt on him.'

When the police arrived on the scene they found Mr Lunn locked in a struggle with a tailor's dummy.

Birmingham police came across two men outside a factory at Willenhall where they were hiding with a torch, a sledgehammer and a pair of gloves. When they were asked what they were up to, the men answered that they were waiting for their girlfriends.

'He is no more dangerous than any other murderer,' was the comforting advice given to newsmen by an Irish detective when he admitted that a man wanted in connection with a recent killing in the Republic had managed to escape from police custody.

FOG AT LUTON

The weather is a favourite topic of conversation in Britain.
It's also a favourite excuse, and it's not just the airlines
who make use of it . . .

When a recent snowfall sent hopeful skiers scurrying
north of the border the local authorities were caught on
the hop. The snow had blocked all the approach roads,
explained a Highlands tourist officer.

☆

There was an all-weather sports field in Ipswich which
had its opening put back six weeks after damage caused
by . . . you've guessed it . . . the weather.

☆

The British aren't alone in employing the forces of nature
to convenient advantage. An RAF pilot about to take off
from Karachi was handed a weather forecast which
seemed to tally with his observations on the ground until
he noticed the date at the top.

'This is six years old,' he complained.

'I know,' said the Met officer laconically, 'but the
weather here never changes.'

☆

A British woman who claimed to have ended droughts
in Asia and South America excused herself from
demonstrating her powers nearer home. 'I could probably flood London tonight,' she admitted, 'but every
time I bring rain something awful happens. Last week
I ended a drought in Guernsey and my washing machine

blew up. When I soaked the Test Match someone hit my car.'

☆

In the middle of the last UK drought in the mid-1970s one local forecaster told the *Portsmouth Evening News*, 'I used to be an amateur weather forecaster, but I went professional because I used to get so many calls from cranks and people who wanted to know when to hang out the washing. There is no doubt in my mind that Mr Callaghan is responsible for the lack of rainfall.'

☆

From the *Saudi Gazette*:

> The weather forecast is cancelled today because of the weather. Forecasts are obtained from the airport, and roads there from our office were impassable. Whether we get the weather tomorrow depends on the weather.

☆

Scrupulous attention to the accuracy of weather forecasting can occasionally lead the unwary into traps. One television forecaster was reported saying, 'We hesitate to say that it is raining, as the Met office doesn't call it that, but the fog is running down the gutters.'

☆

The court of inquiry that looked into the loss of the *Titanic* could not have been surprised to hear the White Star Line cite the weather as the cause of the disaster which claimed over 1,500 lives. But they must have pricked up their ears when the defence blamed the sea for being 'too calm'. Not only the late skipper, Captain Smith, who went down with his ship, but also at least one of the look-outs during that fateful watch had described the sea as being as calm as a millpond.

All the more reason, you might suppose, for the tragedy to have been avoided – but in nautical terms this isn't the case. Seemingly even a minor swell might have saved the ship. Icebergs may be virtually invisible in the North Atlantic nights, but the waves breaking round their base provide adequate warning. Sad to say, there were no waves to be seen on the night of 15 April, 1912.

☆

At the outset of a walk-out in the Navy Department at Bath one of the leaders told journalists, 'If members cannot get in to work tomorrow because of the weather we may have to postpone the walk-out.'

☆

Following the spectacular collapse of his property empire, which went into a £104 million nose-dive in the mid-1970s' property crisis, city financier William Stern knew just where to turn for his poetic inspiration when confronted by reporters. 'The summer was so beautiful,' he told them, 'that no one could believe it would be replaced by a hard Siberian winter.'

Top Twenty Weather Excuses

The car locks are frozen solid and the pipes have burst in the roof so we haven't any hot water to pour over them to get inside the car.

Lightning cut off the electricity and sent the phone haywire.

You know they were forecasting strong gusts. The kitchen window's just blown in all over this evening's dinner.

After that terrible accident on the M6 I took one look at the fog and pulled in to the next service area. You may not have had any your way, but it's when it's patchy that it's most dangerous.

We were hot-air ballooning and picked up a squall which blew us half-way to Norwich.

That sudden downpour has sent a flash flood through the sitting room. We've rescued the furniture but the carpet's a write-off.

I was on my way out when I stepped in a puddle and soaked my feet. By the time I'd changed I knew I was too late.

I couldn't meet your family with prickly heat.

I've had a fog phobia ever since that horror film you persuaded me to see with you.

With all this bad weather I've caught a terrible cold.

We woke up to find the wind had blown down part of the wall and the farmer's Ayrshires were making merry in the vegetable garden.

I forgot to put anti-freeze in the radiator and last night's frost has cracked the engine block.

The storm brought down the power lines. We can't cook. There's no hot water. Everything's defrosted in the fridge, so there's no food. And the electricity board can't connect us until the day after tomorrow.

It's so hot my denture glue keeps melting.

The water will be so rough and you know how queasy my stomach is.

There was so much water on the road that when I hit a puddle the engine just died in the middle. I called the rescue service but you can imagine how busy they were.

I've overdone the sunbathing.

There's something wrong with the solar heating panels and we're worried about the boiler if this heat continues.

There didn't seem any point in coming over to play tennis. It was raining so heavily with us that I knew the courts would be slippery even if it stopped.

They've banned all caravans from the motorway until the weather improves, and that means us as well.

GONE TO LUNCH

With jobs and business hard to come by there's a greater need than ever for business excuses. Whether you're explaining why you're late, having to account for company policy or trying to avoid someone, your job can depend on your excuse.

☆

'I will not have naked flesh on my stand,' asserted the then sales director of the Lotus sports car company at the Motor Show, when explaining the presence of a coloured model clad in a feather boa. 'You have to understand what our car is all about,' he added. 'I won't say that the man who buys one of our yellow dropheads is running a mistress, but he wants to make his friends wonder whether he might be running one. A coloured girl is the great status symbol in mistresses at the moment. It's a subliminal message we are putting across.'

☆

Dismissing the claim that this holiday camp didn't satisfy all its clients, the manager said, 'If things are so bad why didn't I receive any complaints until the last night of the week? There are 900 campers and only 400 have complained.'

☆

'Could I speak to your employer, please?' asked a man confronted with a new secretary.
   'Are you a salesman, a creditor, or a friend of his?'
   'I'm all three.'
   'I'm afraid he's busy in a meeting. He's away on business. Would you like to come this way?'

Excuses of the well-trained secretary

A.M.

'He hasn't come in yet.'
'I'm expecting him at any moment.'
'He's just rung to say he'll be a little late.'
'He's been in, but he's had to go out again.'
'He's gone to lunch.'

P.M.

'I expect he'll be in at any moment.'
'He's not back yet. Can I take a message?'
'He must be somewhere in the building. His things are in the office.'
'Yes, he was in a minute ago, but he went out again.'
'I don't know whether he'll be back or not.'
'No, he's gone for the day.'

☆

Commenting on what appeared to be their racist attitude, a former public relations official of British Railways

Western Region said, 'We don't have a colour bar – it is just a question of colour preference.'

☆

A black school-leaver was turned down by a prospective employer who told him, 'Your pigmentation would make you more allergic to frostbite in our frozen food.'

☆

The chairman of a British company with important international interests noted with concern that his South African subsidiary had sent in some very dubious figures in the annual report. He asked for an audited report of the total payroll and spotted the cause of the disparity immediately. Among the list of employees there were none with obviously Bantu names. He asked the South African company to explain this apparent omission. They replied that Bantu employees were not classified as manpower. They were listed under Fixtures and Fittings.

☆

The art of the euphemism is not unknown in business circles. Some years ago *Metal Progress* and *Shipbuilding & Shipping Record* catalogued some of the choicest examples that had come to light alongside a revealing glossary. Any aspiring tycoon would do well to study it . . .

Glossary

Three of the examples were chosen for detailed study	The results on the others didn't make sense and were ignored
The results will be reported at a later date	I might possibly get round to this sometime
It might be argued that . . .	I have such a good answer to this objection that I shall now raise it

Correct within an order of magnitude	Wrong
Although some detail has been lost in reproduction, it is clear from the original micrograph that . . .	It is impossible to tell from the micrograph
The most reliable values are those of Jones	He was a student of mine
Typical results are shown	The best results are shown
. . . accidentally strained during mounting	. . . dropped on the floor
. . . handled with extreme care throughout the experiments	. . . not dropped on the floor
It is clear that much additional work will be required before a complete understanding . . .	I don't understand it
It is hoped that this work will stimulate further work in the field	This paper isn't very good, but neither is any of the others on this miserable subject
The agreement with the predicted curve is: . . . excellent . . . good . . . satisfactory . . . fair	 Fair Poor Doubtful Imaginary

I thought I told you.

I was going to finish that job first thing but the head of department shifted me to something else.

I was dealing with a client at the time.

No one told me to go ahead.

That's not my department.

There must have been a computer error.

This scheme will need a lot more study before we can go through with it.

That's the way we've always done it.

I forgot. Wouldn't you with the amount of work at the moment?

How was I to know this was different?

With all the cuts in staff in this department is it surprising?

That's his job, not mine.

The photocopier packed up and I had to chase all over the building to find a free one.

I didn't think it was that important.

I'm still waiting for the go-ahead.

Why bother? The old man won't buy it.

How could I finish it off when the original's nowhere to be seen. It's time someone organized the filing system.

I didn't know you were in a hurry.

Wait until the boss comes back and ask him.

No one showed me how to do it.

HYPOCHONDRIACS ANONYMOUS

Medical excuses have been so overplayed that it now takes real imagination and ingenuity to make them stick. Flu, tummy bugs, pains in the back and period pains no longer cut any ice. Any excuse based on ill-health needs to be exotic or carefully worked out.

Skin-deep Excuses

These are the ones guaranteed to put off the most ardent suitors or persuade the most ferocious boss that you're better left in self-imposed quarantine.

I've come up with a boil on the end of my nose. It looks about ready to burst.

We tried a new fish restaurant and now I've come up in hives – huge, sticky patches all over my face and body. The doctor's given me some ointment and I've got to spend most of the time in the shade.

A sty has blown my left eye up as big as a cherry. I hope the hot poultices I'm using will sort it out.

Would you mind waiting until I shake off the ringworm?

I know it isn't acne but it doesn't make me feel any better. Can you imagine what shaving's like?

They say I've got eczema. It's brought on by emotional problems. I've got big, scaly sores all over, and even the calamine lotion can't get rid of the itching.

My ear got inflamed and now it looks as if I've just stepped out of the ring after going fifteen rounds.

Top Twenty Medical Excuses

These are the all-purpose ones. If they can be dressed up with convincing props or some accurate information on treatment and prescriptions, so much the better.

I got bitten by a squirrel on holiday. After that recent rabies case the local hospital's taking no chances. The treatment sounds ghastly.

They want a semen specimen to see how the vasectomy's worked out, but they forgot to give me any dirty pictures. I've got to go over there straight away to get on with it.

I've been passing blood for a couple of days.

I've been haemorrhaging from my new coil.

My breasts have been inflamed for a week. Mastitis? Is that what it's called?

My piles are at it again. I didn't get a wink of sleep. They've given me that gooey stuff to make the motion easier, but it's still agony. I'm just praying they don't have to operate.

There's been a terrible pain in my cheek. The dentist says one of the bicuspids has an abscess. I've got to have root canal treatment. That can be hell, so don't expect me until next week.

I'd love to come but my doctor says that any alcohol will only make my canker sores worse.

I was carrying the turkey out of the freezer when it slipped and fell on my foot. I know I shouldn't have been wearing slippers, but my big toe is twice its normal size and I can't walk on it. My wife's just getting the car to take me to Casualty. (This will require a bandaged foot and walking-stick when you return to work.)

I haven't liked to make a fuss but I've been constipated for a week and now the sickness and headaches have become so bad I've been told to stay at home for a day or two. The doctor wants me to take enemas, drink gallons of fluids and do some exercises.

You probably didn't know that I've had to wear orthopaedic shoes for a while. Well, last night they disappeared at the local baths and now I can't walk for five minutes without shooting pains up my back. I can't move until I get another pair.

We decided to try *coitus interruptus* and this morning I was sick and fainted. My husband wants me to have a pregnancy test right away.

You know they said my last trip wasn't in a malaria zone? They were wrong.

The dentist had to take out a wisdom tooth. It was pretty bad and he doped me up so much that I still haven't come down to earth.

38

I'd love to come, but this toothache started too late for me to make the dentist's surgery, so I bought a quarter bottle of whisky and now I'm in no state to drive.

I broke my dentures. Not only can't I eat but I look like a goldfish. Could we make it another time?

I've lost a contact lens. I know it's here somewhere, but I can't see a thing without it and it always takes me a couple of days to adjust to wearing glasses again.

They've found a lump. They say it's nothing to worry about, but it's being investigated immediately.

The kids have just got over mumps and I'm not feeling too good myself. I don't believe these old wives' tales, but the doctor doesn't want me taking any chances. I've got to go in right away.

Heaven knows how I caught it, but they've diagnosed hepatitis. (Watch this excuse. By rights you should stay off the booze for six months at least!)

IN NEED OF MODERNIZATION

The very phrase should sound alarm bells, but how many of us move house often enough to learn from past mistakes? The estate agent's blurb, the excitement of a new home and the prospect of getting away from the neighbours throw up a smokescreen which only clears after we move in. I know the number of times I've been carried away by reading about houses only to be bitterly disappointed by the reality. Here are a few extracts from the estate agent's vocabulary to watch out for:

Unusual location	In the path of projected motorway
Local authority grants available	About to be condemned
Period residence	Built at least two years ago
Select neighbourhood	Beside sewage works
Compact	Tiny
Country gentleman's residence	No longer considered suitable for agricultural tenants
Unusual features	No roof
Delightful rural location	In flight path of nuclear bomber base
Box room	Suitable for accommodating one or two large cardboard boxes (folded)

A wealth of period features	Timber infestation by every bug that's ever enjoyed wood, ceilings on which to brain yourself, dry rot, rising damp and an electrical circuit best operated in rubber gloves and wellies
Quiet, secluded setting	On site of proposed dormitory town
Well situated	In full view of the neighbours
Within easy distance of local amenities	Next door to pub and opposite sex shop
Rare opportunity to buy	No one else wants it
For the gardening enthusiast	Grounds like a jungle
Extensively modernized	Former DIY owner had a breakdown under the strain
Unspoilt	Planning permission granted for field next door
Deceptive appearance	It looks terrible
Partial central heating	The room above the boiler can get quite warm in summer
Easily maintained	Requires at least two gardeners and living-in maid

Useful outbuildings   No interior WC

Much sought after	It's been on the market at least twice before and still no one wants it
En suite bathroom	Wash-basin in corner (a shower if you're lucky)
By private treaty	If it went to auction it would never reach the reserve
Owner eager to sell	If it goes within a week the subsidence cracks won't be noticed
Carefully maintained	No building society has ever granted a mortgage on it without insisting on major structural repairs
Subject to new instructions	They've just discovered death watch beetle
Sold	Unless you offer a higher price

JOHNSON AND FRIENDS

Dr Johnson was more one to deflate the excuses of others than to offer his own. When he and Boswell met for the first time, the latter, knowing of the doctor's views on those from north of the border, said, 'Dr Johnson, I do indeed come from Scotland, but I can't help it.'

Johnson replied, 'That, sir, I find is what a great many of your countrymen cannot help.'

There were, however, rare occasions when Johnson made an excuse of his own, albeit a guarded one. When challenged by a hectoring hostess to say what he thought of music and whether he agreed that it was the most satisfying of arts, he replied, 'No, madam, but of all noises, I think music is the least disagreeable.'

Other famous names had more urgent reasons for coming out with their excuses. Chico Marx, caught by his wife kissing a chorus girl, told her, 'I wasn't kissing her. I was whispering in her mouth.' And Isadora Duncan, discovered by a friend *in flagrante delicto* with her chauffeur, said, 'He's a greek god in disguise.'

Here, then, is a selection of the excuses of the great and famous drawn from their correspondence, memoirs and friends . . .

'The finest woman in nature would not detain me an hour from you; but you must sometimes suffer the rivalship of the wisest of men.'

Sir Richard Steele – *Letters to His Wife*

☆

'There is the greatest practical benefit in making a few failures early in life.'

Thomas Huxley

☆

'I've made it a rule never to drink by daylight and never to refuse a drink after dark.'

H.L. Mencken

☆

'A reputation is a great noise. The greater noise you make, the farther off you are heard. Laws, institutions, monuments, nations, all fall. But the noise continues and resounds in after ages.'

Napoleon Bonaparte

☆

'I have said and done all that I could; I have made proposal after proposal to Britain; likewise to France. These proposals were always ridiculed – rejected with scorn. However, when I saw that the other side intended to fight, I naturally . . . forged a powerful weapon of defence.'

Adolf Hitler

☆

'I'm the only President you've got.'

Lyndon Johnson

☆

'Why should I be ashamed? I never took anything to help myself. I was merely collecting political contributions, and even then, I wasn't collecting them directly, the way some of the testimonies say.'

Spiro Agnew

☆

'All our fifth columnists have been liquidated in the purge.'
Joseph Stalin, 1938

☆

'The rugged mountains and the muddy valleys of that country are not adapted to our kind of fighting.'

Benito Mussolini (on the humiliating retreat of his army from its Albanian stronghold of Koritza)

☆

'I have found it impossible to carry the heavy burden of responsibility and to discharge my duties as King as I would wish to do without the help and support of the woman I love.'

The Duke of Windsor (Edward VIII)

☆

'What is the throne? – a bit of wood gilded and covered with velvet. I am the state – I alone am here the representative of the people. Even if I had done wrong you should not have reproached me in public – people wash their dirty linen at home. France has more need of me than I of France.'

Ivan the Terrible

☆

'The car overturned in a deep pond and immediately filled with water. I remember thinking as the cold water rushed in around my head that I was, for certain, drowning. But somehow I struggled to the surface alive. I made immediate and repeated efforts to save Mary Jo by diving into the strong and murky current, but succeeded only in increasing my state of utter exhaustion and alarm.'

Edward Kennedy

☆

'Again I must complain of Indolence: she is a tyrant who oppresses me, who confines me in bed as criminals are confined in their cells. In vain I try to rise. I am weighted down with the heaviest of fetters. I have freedom of motion only to stretch my legs and fold my arms; my very eyes appear to be held shut with fine chains. What witchcraft!'

James Boswell

☆

'My Dear Lady Holland, I have not the heart, when an amiable lady says, "Come to *Semiramis* in my box" to decline; but I get bolder at a distance. *Semiramis* would be to me pure misery. I love music very little – I hate acting; I have the worst opinion of *Semiramis* herself, and the whole thing (I cannot help it) seems so childish and foolish that I cannot abide it. Moreover, it would be rather out of etiquette for a Canon of St Paul's to go to an opera, and where etiquette prevents me from things disagreeable to myself, I am a perfect martinet. All these things considered, I am sure you will not be a *Semiramis* to me, but let me off.'

Sydney Smith

☆

'The only way to get rid of a temptation is to yield to it.'
Oscar Wilde

☆

'Order, with regard to places for things, papers, etc., I found extremely difficult to acquire. I had not been early accustomed to it, and, having an exceeding good memory, I was not so sensible of the inconvenience attending want of method.'

Benjamin Franklin

☆

'It is probably true that the majority of wild Indians have no inherited tendencies whatever towards morality or chastity, according to an enlightened standard. Chastity and morality among them must come from education and contact with the better element of the whites.'

W. A. Jones, US Commissioner of Indian Affairs, 1903

☆

'As Chinese troops have recently shown frequent signs of movement along the northern frontier of French Indo-China bordering on China, Japanese troops, with the object of mainly taking precautionary measures, have been reinforced to a certain extent in the northern part of French Indo-China. As a natural sequence of this step, certain movements have been made among the troops stationed in the southern part of the said territory. It seems that an exaggerated report has been made of these movements.'

Japanese ambassador to the US (two days before the attack on Pearl Harbor)

☆

'In our history books we pay tribute to the man with the gun. He won the American Revolution and the War of 1812. He defended democracy in 1917–18. He fought the greatest global war in history in 1941–45. The American with a gun has been a great stabilizing influence in maintaining a balance of world power. Between the wars, the National Rifle Association has been primary guardian of the American rifleman tradition which becomes so vital in time of war.'

A spokesman for the US National Rifle Association

☆

'Twelve hundred thousand, according to the best authority.'
'Good heavens.'
'Yes, sir, twelve hundred thousand – no doubt of it. You see, all of our generals, when they get whipped, say the enemy outnumbers them from three to five to one, and I must believe them. We have four hundred thousand men in the field, and three times four make twelve. Do you see it?'

Abraham Lincoln (asked by a journalist how many men the Confederation had in the field)

48

KIDS' STUFF

Children and excuses go hand in hand. You're either listening to the ones they trot out, or you're scratching about for one that will wash them. On rare occasions the kids themselves form a perfect excuse to get you out of difficulties.

Top Twenty Children's Excuses

How can I get to sleep when you're watching television?

Everyone else is allowed to . . .

I'm scared to walk to school because that bully's waiting for me.

He forced me to do it.

You always treat   r better than me.

It's too hot/cold to wear that.

Nobody told me the 'f' word was naughty.

I don't feel very well.

The teacher gave us the homework, but didn't explain
how to do it.

The teacher said we had to watch it.

It's got lumps in it

Why have I got to . . . no one else has to.

You promised me I could watch it until nine.

Daddy/Mummy promised me I could watch it.

My friend's parents don't mind her doing it and she's
younger than me.

If you don't let me, people will think you're old-fashioned.

The last time you bought something for me 'to grow into'
everyone at school laughed at me.

I can't get to sleep without it.

You keep contradicting yourself.

Every time I fall asleep he comes in and wakes me up.

Top Twenty Excuses to Children

You aren't old enough.

I'll only change my mind when you change your behaviour.

You know your father doesn't like that sort of film.

You can't have that now because that's what Father Christmas is bringing you.

No more . . . you have to learn to share.

I wasn't given a bicycle until I was thirteen and then I had to pay for a quarter of it out of my pocket money.

You're much too big a boy for that.

It's for your own good.

You can only watch that film with an adult and we're both tied up for the rest of the week.

I'll have to discuss it with your father/mother first.

Your father/mother is against it.

I don't mind you going . . . once you've done all your work here.

You don't look very well to me. I think you'd better stay inside.

Granny would be terribly disappointed if you didn't try and eat some of her crumble . . . and your birthday isn't that far away.

It's very good for you. It's full of vitamins.

Superman eats it.

That's too rich for you. You'll enjoy the sausages and chips much more.

We made it specially for you.

The place we're going to has a bar which means you won't be allowed inside.

Daddy's allowed to do that because he's grown up now. When he was your age he wasn't allowed to do it.

Top Twenty Children's Excuses – to get you off the hook

Our baby sitter had an accident on the way over here and it's too late to find another.

Sorry we missed your party. Jamie made a paper glider out of the invitation.

They were playing petrol stations and now there are four gallons of water in the car's fuel tank.

They're watching television and I have to be ready to cut out the violence.

I promised I'd assemble the swing they got for Christmas. You know what I'm like. It'll take all week-end.

She is two hours late coming home from school. I must go and look for her.

David has just discovered matches. I can't leave until the babysitter arrives.

He opened my briefcase and found my copy of *Playboy*. That 'facts-of-life' talk has come on me sooner than expected.

He's been in a fight and the other boy's father is coming round to sort it out.

They've been teaching him this new maths at school and he's asked me to help him with his homework. I can't make head or tail of it, so I've got to study the book while he's in bed.

The children dropped the car keys down the waste-disposal and I'm in the middle of taking it to pieces.

We promised them we'd go to the zoo and tomorrow looks like being the first fine day.

They've both gone down with chicken pox.

He can't keep anything down and I'm waiting for the doctor to ring back. I may have to take him to surgery right away.

They've been staying with friends who keep chickens. I don't know what they picked up, they haven't stopped scratching. I'm washing all their clothes now and my husband's got them in the bath.

Simon ate the laxative chocolate by mistake.

Andy tried to make a pet out of a rat he found near the dustbin. His appointment at the surgery is in twenty minutes.

It's the night of the school play. He's only got two lines but we couldn't miss them.

The school just rang to say he's concussed himself in the gym. They've called an ambulance, but they want me to go to the hospital.

We'd love to, but it's half-term.

LEGAL AND BINDING

'The life of the law', wrote that great American judge, Oliver Wendell Holmes, 'has not been logic; it has been experience,' which is just as well judging by some of the excuses heard in courtrooms.

☆

A Carlisle man who stripped his wife, stuffed her mouth full of clothes, bound her hands behind her back and hit her, explained his action as a desperate attempt to show that their marriage was not over.

☆

For contravening the regulations that limited fishermen to a maximum of six hooks to every line, a Greek fisherman was taken to court in Sutherland charged with using a line almost three quarters of a mile long to which were attached 230 hooks. He had been fishing in the dark, he told the court, and hadn't been able to count the hooks!

☆

The fright of his life was put forward by a Nottinghamshire licensee as the excuse for a moment's erratic driving on the county's A606. He had been driving along normally, he told the court, when a goat suddenly jumped on to the seat beside him. This unexpected arrival caused him momentarily to lose control and he drove the wrong way round a traffic island.

☆

A solicitor at a loss for words when in court defending a client told the bench in desperation, 'The first my client knew of the accident was when it occurred.'

☆

An Aberdeen man who had caused some alarm in a local bar by burying a hatchet in the wooden surface while drinking there explained, 'I was having difficulty in catching the barmaid's eye.'

☆

A solicitor representing Havering Council in a court action some years ago tried to reject a prosecution witness's evidence on the grounds that it was inadmissible. 'I think my friend is disturbed because the witness has taken the oath on a steak and kidney pie,' he told the court.

☆

A Scottish sheriff was informed by a poacher, brought before him charged with killing a pheasant, that he had shot the bird because it had been looking tired.

☆

The owner of a hotel on the Isle of Man was found guilty by a Manx court of contravening the licensing laws. The court ruled that by joining in with her customers as they sang songs she had willingly entered into an entertainment for which the hotel was not licensed. Had she kept her mouth shut, there would have been no case to answer, she was told. The court fined her ten shillings.

☆

A divorce was granted to a Danish woman after a court heard how her husband had stripped her and chased her through the streets, slapping her bottom with a heavy sausage – because she had burned his supper.

☆

A defendant brought before magistrates in Harrogate used as his excuse the news that he had been made a permanent civil servant. 'I could think of nothing else,' he told the bench. 'I had just got everything I wanted in life.'

☆

A man who was fined £10 by a court in Fleetwood after being found guilty of stealing fish told the court that he had only taken the fish to pay off another £10 fine which he had been given earlier for receiving stolen fish.

☆

A Middlesborough solicitor asked the city's police court to excuse his client from attending a forthcoming hearing saying, 'In the first place he is a man of not very bright intellect, and secondly, he is employed on important government work.'

☆

Simon Naysmith, an unemployed accountant who appeared as the defendant in a West Country hearing was asked whether he had bought a sack of manure for £3 and had later resold it for £650. He agreed that he had, adding, 'Mark-ups are normal in any profession.'

☆

Leamington magistrates heard from a housewife, brought before them accused of shoplifting two tins of meat, that she had 'never been the same' since the shock of seeing a man running about in the nude. 'I've been under sedatives from my doctor ever since,' she said.

☆

When a senior judge was told that a 25-year-old man's sex life had been affected by an accident with a bulldozer, he asked if the man was married. Hearing that he wasn't, the judge stated that he therefore couldn't see how the accident could affect him.

In answer to a summons for an affiliation order a Berkshire man replied by letter, 'I don't know whether or not I'm the father of the child. I'm only an apprentice.'

Pleading guilty to having given a false name to the policemen who arrested him, a student, named Alan Smith, told the magistrates in Hartlepool, 'I didn't think they would believe my name was Smith because I had no identification on me, so I told them it was Jones.'

☆

Following complaints from female patients, a Dutch optician was sent for trial in 1979 charged with various offences that amounted to unprofessional conduct. In the course of the trial it was revealed that women who went to him for treatment were asked to remove their clothes and dance around his consulting-room while he played an accordion. In his client's defence the lawyer told the court, 'This test was carried out to make sure that they were the right kind for contact lenses.'

MARRIAGE LINES

Married life calls for a special brand of excuses. From getting hitched to the final divorce hearing, via forgotten anniversaries and petty squabbles 'Marriage', as Vicki Baum said, 'always demands the greatest understanding of the art of insincerity possible between two human beings'.

☆

A young Welsh carpenter, Derek Jones, had the misfortune to fall for a girl with a passion for foreigners. In order to win her affection he told a bit of a white lie and said that he was the son of a Puerto Rican uranium miner. As he later explained, 'For two years she has known me as Nassa. Whenever we went out I had to pick places where I was unknown. But there were always people around who used to shout 'Hullo Derek' and things like that. Finally, I decided to get a document that would prove who I was, but it was my undoing.' (He was fined £18 for trying to obtain a passport in the name of Nassa Ocovish.)

☆

A 32-year-old woman arrested for soliciting on the eve of her wedding night pleaded that she had no choice. Without that night's earnings she wouldn't have been able to buy a wedding present for her husband.

☆

Cupid's arrow struck a West Virginian man late in life when at the age of 102 he popped the question to a slip of a girl forty years his junior. Applying for a marriage licence he discounted the likelihood of their starting a family with the remark, 'My eyes are giving me trouble.'

☆

The privacy of marital squabbles assumed a ludicrous dimension when lodger Brian James heard a shot but didn't leave his bedroom to investigate. It turned out that his landlord had just shot his wife, but Mr James remained unmoved by the incident even when giving evidence at the trial. 'I assumed that Mrs Dick was being assaulted,' he said, 'and I had no wish to get involved.'

☆

An Inspector of Taxes sent a query to one tax-payer asking whether the housekeeper mentioned on his tax return was a relative. The man replied, 'Well, not exactly, but she was my wife before I divorced her.'

☆

At the age of 82 a retired Baptist minister decided he couldn't stand his wife any longer and took out divorce proceedings. In stating his grounds he cited his wife's infuriating habit of praying aloud in Welsh. 'When I asked her to pray in English – if she had to pray aloud – she resented it,' he added.

☆

The theft of one hundredweight of liquid chocolate was justified by a man whose wife had just obtained a separation order, as a last ditch attempt to patch up their marriage. She liked chocolate, he said, so he thought he would get her some.

☆

'The quality of the cooking is an important part of marriage,' pronounced a French judge, clearing a Parisian husband of the charge of murder but imposing an eight year sentence for manslaughter. The man had made no attempt to disguise his guilt, partly as this was the second occasion on which he had been charged with killing his wife. His first marriage ended when he did away with his good lady after she consistently undercooked his steak. Twelve years later wife number two followed her predecessor for overcooking her husband's steak.

☆

A call girl who turned out to be the wife of a colonel explained her choice of profession with the remark, 'I only do this to pay my husband's surtax.'

☆

Such was the stigma attached to TB fifty years ago that the wife of a fairly well-to-do Scot preferred to tell her neighbours that he was in prison rather than admit that he was at a sanatorium undergoing treatment for TB.

Excuses for forgetting birthdays, anniversaries, etc.

I wanted your present to have a special wrapping but when I went to collect it the shop was closed. They didn't tell me today was their half-day.

The anniversary isn't until tomorrow! I'll get the licence to prove it. (You do this and, finding you're wrong, offer to drive back to the office to fetch the present. With luck she'll settle for a cheap meal out.)

I thought we could celebrate Valentine's Day with a bottle of wine and an early night. How about it?

It wasn't until this morning that I remembered that you'd been given an identical present last Christmas. Since you never use it/wear it I knew you wouldn't want another. They let me change it for something much more suitable, but the right one's out of stock until next week. Can we keep it a surprise until then?

When I collected it they gave me the wrong one. I'd bought you a piece of jewellery and the package I collected had come from the hardware department. They're looking into it, but I can't have a refund or replacement until they've sorted out the mess.

It's not that I forgot, but I've noticed how sensitive you've been recently about your age and I thought it might be best not to remind you you're a year older.

Excuses for marriage breakdowns

She always waited until we were in bed to tell me about her day's shopping and her plans for tomorrow.

His parents never recovered from his marrying me.

She couldn't accept my superior intelligence.

It was cheaper than sending in a joint tax return.

She told all our friends about my bed-wetting.

He decided the children should be brought up as Moonies.

The only way to arouse her was to beat her up.

He never bought me flowers in twelve years of marriage.

She became a Jehovah's Witness.

He didn't like it when I went back to work at the massage parlour.

She passed her law exams and started earning more than me.

He snored like a fog horn.

She started reading feminist books.

He spent all his money in 'adult' book shops.

Excuses for avoiding jobs about the house

They say that jobs like that are best done by professionals.

You know how clumsy I am. Whenever I wash up I always break something.

It would be better to wait until it rains before we start trying to repair leaks in the roof.

You should have asked me to carry out the dustbin before I changed into my best suit.

If we wait until it's really dirty it will save on detergent.

I'd like to, but what would people think if they saw us working in the garden on Good Friday?

If I tried to do it with the weather as it is, the door/window would only shrink during the next dry spell.

It would be stupid to wash the car on a day like this. It would end up more blotched and speckled than it is already.

I lent the right tool to a colleague and he's just gone on leave for a fortnight.

With a back like mine it would be madness to lift it.

NOT THE DONE THING

The commonest excuses are the ones we make about our behaviour. Most people prefer to avoid giving offence but we all commit social gaffes sometimes. We'd hardly be human if we didn't.

There was a guest at a grand dinner who absentmindedly drank the contents of her finger bowl and then excused herself by saying that she thought it was clear lemon soup.

A London surgeon who was told by his landlord that he was an undesirable tenant took his case to the Marylebone Rent Tribunal where the landlord was asked to substantiate his claim. After pointing out that the house was situated in Upper Berkeley Street, the landlord said, 'He does his own shopping. It is detrimental for this class of house for people to carry shopping. It is not liked by the tenants.'

'Jesus forgives you,' born-again Christian Chris Connor told John Weyman after the latter had just pushed a chocolate pudding in his face.
'Jesus told me to hit you with a pie because you are a fraud,' Weyman told him.

Journalists on a Fleet Street paper were incensed to read a headline in a rival publication that said, 'Asian father of 12 on £100 a week social security', so they wrote a letter of complaint. The managing editor wrote back saying that if the word Asian hadn't been included the readers would have thought that the man in question was Irish.

When a Birmingham nurse was dismissed from one of the city's hospitals for spitting in front of the matron she told a hospital tribunal that she had been courteously removing her chewing gum before speaking to her superior.

☆

When one of India's leading film stars, Tendra Jay, was asked how he justified his own standard of living in comparison with the poverty all around him, he replied, 'I'm not in favour of communism. I don't encourage beggary. What I can't stand is the disparity in incomes. I try to bridge it by employing as many servants as possible at high salaries. Disparity really gets me.'

☆

When it was agreed to turn the Silence room, the Truro Room, in the House of Lords Library into a no-smoking room, there was at least one peer who wasn't happy with the new arrangements. 'I shall continue to smoke in that room. No one will be able to stop me because if anyone speaks I will say it is a Silence Room,' he announced to the House.

☆

During a golf club competition a retired colonel who was notorious for his abusive language was drawn against another member who was equally notorious for his disapproval of strong words. The colonel had been prevailed upon to keep his tongue in check, which he did successfully for the first seven holes. However, a sliced drive on the eighth tee threw him into a violent rage and he bellowed a four-letter word across the course. Seeing the look of horror on his opponent's face he hurried over and said apologetically, 'I do beg your pardon. I meant to say "bugger" '.

☆

In later life the great F. E. Smith, then Lord Birkenhead, got into the habit of popping in to the Athenaeum Club on his way back to the House of Lords, after lunching in the Café Royal, to 'spend a penny'. After a while certain members of the club decided he had taken the liberty of using their loo uninvited once too often and pressured the club secretary to tackle him the next time he appeared.

'Lord Birkenhead, are you a member of this club?' the secretary asked him after his next visit to the gents.

Gazing round the magnificent hall with its Greek pillars, marble staircase and fine paintings, with a look of surprise, Lord Birkenhead replied, 'Oh, it's a club as well, is it?'

☆

ᴑ celebrate her wedding anniversary in a special way Mrs Winifred Lunt of Ipswich took up a pop singer's recent offer to perform in the homes of his fans and arranged for him to entertain her husband with his latest number. Mr Lunt, to whom the singer's arrival was a total surprise, was alarmed to find a drunk man on his doorstep demanding to be let in. After spending twenty minutes in the lavatory the singer emerged and demanded a tennis racket with which to mime the song. No sooner had he started singing than the neighbours began knocking on the wall in protest. He replied by knocking on the Lunts' wall with his racket and shouting swear words up the chimney. His parting shot was to throw up all over the hall carpet as he left. When Mrs Lunt told him that he had ruined their evening his answer was, 'That's show-business.'

☆

When the organizer of a church charity raffle was apprehended drilling a hole in the wall that divided male and female lavatories he tried to bluff his way out by saying, 'I had just bought a Bumper Tool outfit and couldn't wait until I got home to try it out.'

☆

Queen Victoria had been on the throne for almost forty years before serious steps were taken to prevent the overflow of untreated sewage into the nation's waterways. So it was with remarkable presence of mind that the Master of Trinity College, Cambridge, replied to his young sovereign when she asked him from a bridge over the Cam what were all the pieces of paper floating on the surface: 'Those, Your Majesty,' he said, 'are notices saying that bathing is forbidden.'

☆

An American sitting on a bar-stool one evening was suddenly stabbed from behind. The victim was just able to turn round and noticed a look of horror on his assailant's face. 'I'm sorry,' said the latter, 'I thought you were someone else.'

OWZAT!

Sports enthusiasts never seem satisfied to let others make up their own minds about their particular sport. They're either trying to make excuses for taking part in it or, more often, trying to explain their own shortcomings.

'We may not be the greatest at winning Winter Olympics,' admitted Squadron Leader Mike Freeman, bobsleigher and flag-bearer at the 1972 Games, 'but at least we can carry our bloody flag properly.'

☆

Writing to the *Field* in defence of bloodsports one correspondent stated that, 'If foxes could hear all sides of the debate on hunting I think they would vote solidly for its continuance.'

☆

Just past the half-way stage in a gruelling boxing match American manager, Angelo Dundee, gave a few words of encouragement to his boy in the ring. The fighter looked wearily at his manager and told him his legs were killing him. 'That's a very good sign,' replied Dundee. 'It means you're getting your second wind.'

☆

When Brighton police arrested an Iranian student, found up to his knees in the sea brandishing a chair leg studded with four-inch nails, they were naturally curious as to what he was up to and why he was in possession of what they described as an 'offensive weapon'. The court, too, was interested to hear what the student had to say for himself, though he remained disarmingly composed throughout the proceedings. 'This is no weapon,' he said. 'It is a bat used in the popular Arabian beach sport of ho-ho. The rules are similar to rounders.' When asked why, in that case, the police had apprehended him in the sea during a snow-storm, he replied, 'The weather was unsuitable for ho-ho, so I decided to club a few fish.'

A remarkable case of sex discrimination occurred a few years ago when the governing body of conker fighting ruled that women would be excluded from the draw for the sixty-four places in the annual world championships to be held at Ashton, Northamptonshire. Defending this decision the chairman of the organizing committee told reporters, 'The event would be ridiculed if it was open to women.'

A visitor to a Home Counties golf club was given precedence on the first tee by four club members who noticed that he was playing with the secretary. After taking his stance the man made a couple of practise swings and then launched a fearsome drive at the ball – missing it by several inches. Three similar shots followed during which the club foursome became increasingly exasperated. Before taking his fifth shot the visitor turned to them and smiling wanly said, 'I'm sorry, gentlemen. The problem is my course is three inches higher than this one.'

A dentist with a passion for golf left a message with his receptionist that he was out all morning and that she was to give her usual reply to any enquiries. The lady had become rather tired of covering for her truant boss and when one of his regular patients asked to see him she modified the stock reply by saying, 'I'm sorry, madam,

I'm afraid he's out on a special case. He has eighteen cavities to fill and says that it will take him all the morning.'

☆

Following a recent case of hunt sabotage in which one of the protestors was horsewhipped by a mounted opponent, the Master of the Hunt expressed his own views on the incident. In his opinion whipping a saboteur fell into the same category as wife-beating. 'They are both private matters between individuals with strong views on the same subject,' he said.

Top Twenty Sporting Excuses

The pitch was muddy.

I'm always best playing in the centre.

That umpire made some of the Indian ones look impartial.

I've been working too hard to play this class of football/rugger/tennis/cricket/squash without wearing myself out.

I need a few more games to get used to this new racquet/bat/rule.

I need a few more games to get over my last injury.

Some of us have full-time jobs to do when we're not playing matches.

This river's been over-fished. The only way you can catch anything is with dynamite.

The sun was in my eyes for most of the game.

Even our best players found it rough out there.

My mind wasn't on it.

I made the mistake of wearing a new pair of boots/tennis shoes/squash shoes without breaking them in first.

I should have stuck to hockey.

Did you see how he tried to spike me on the final bend?

With the pitch in that state you needed four legs to stay upright.

They filled us with drink before the game and stuck to soft drinks themselves. I had double vision until half-time.

I can't concentrate when there are people talking all round the course.

We've got a new coach who doesn't understand our game at all.

Something went in my left leg after I'd been out there five minutes but I had to keep going.

Winning is so futile. I always play for the fun of it.

PUBLIC WORKS

Town Councils, the Post Office, Telecom and the rest of the public service have become so used to criticism that they've got their excuses down to a fine art.

A Cheshire man dialled Directory Enquiries and asked for the number of a firm called Alpha Cleaning Services. He was told that no such number was listed; could he spell the name? A second search revealed the number which was given with the tart observation, 'If it's not spelled normally you're meant to tell us, you know!'

☆

Mrs Denise Hawker collected her post one morning and found a grubby envelope together with a note from the Post Office saying that it had been chewed by snails during transit.

☆

Corporal punishment has always been a hot potato in education circles. Many of those involved in the process in the Walsall area were alarmed to discover that the tawse had been administered in just one school five hundred times in five years. Challenged with these findings the chairman of the education committee defended the policy, saying that it seemed appropriate in view of the town's strong links with the leather trade.

☆

During a discussion on the change to comprehensive education in Warrington one Councillor Stirrup remarked, 'I am not against comprehensive education but

I want it within the grammar school framework.'

☆

Refusing a local education authority's application to employ a school crossing patrol at a new site, the Ministry of Transport decided that there was not sufficient demand for the crossing and that it would only be used by children in any case.

☆

Marylebone Council turned down an application by the Anti-Vivisection League to use premises in Harley Street on the grounds that the proposed use would be out of keeping with the character of the area.

☆

From an issue of *London Post*, the journal of the London District Council of the Union of Post Office Workers.

We regret that due to the loss in the post of all the copy, the first proof for this edition of *London Post*, the publication of this issue has been unavoidably delayed.
We apologize to our readers, and hope that postal services will be more reliable in the future.

☆

Following a review of rural deliveries a Derbyshire vicar received his mail one morning and asked the postman whether in future there was to be only one daily delivery. 'Oh no,' said the postman, 'you'll still be getting two deliveries a day, it's just that we'll be bringing them both together.'

☆

The alphabetical list of subscribers in an Ulster telephone directory began mysteriously with the name O'Kane, P and Company. Giving the Post Office's version of the mistake a spokesman attempted to cast light on the problem by saying, 'Well you see it was a wrong input into the computer. The girl fed in the figure nought instead of the letter O – I'm so sorry, I mean she fed in the letter O instead of the figure nought. Over here, the figures come before letters of the alphabet, if you see what I mean . . .'

☆

A Cornish resident was taking a walk one chill winter morning when his attention was drawn to the antics of a group of council workmen clearing the road. Two men were busily brushing snow from the road into the gutter, while two others following behind methodically shovelled the snow from the gutter into the road. Unable to contain his curiosity the bystander asked why there was this apparent conflict in purpose. 'The others are town men,' one of the sweepers told him. 'We come under the County.'

☆

An application by Bridport Rural District Council to build a dozen old people's bungalows was rejected by many local residents, among whom was a man who argued against the plan saying, 'There is nowhere to park hearses.'

☆

A Redditch ratepayer applied to his urban council for permission to erect a telegraph pole in his garden. The application was laid before the Estates, Baths and Cemeteries Committee who postponed making a definite decision until they had investigated the option of moving the man and his family to a house already fitted with a telegraph pole.

☆

Following the death of a seventy-year-old tenant of a

local authority old people's bungalow, her relatives received a demand for four weeks' rent in lieu of notice. A spokesman for Peterborough Rural Council explained that four weeks' notice was required before any property could be vacated.

A former mayor of Lincoln replied to critics of the city's housing policy, 'There is no housing shortage in Lincoln today – just a rumour put about by people who have nowhere to live.'

Widespread disappointment greeted the news that a public drinking fountain installed in Walton-on-the-Naze would not be able to operate to its full potential. The council told the residents that the cost of connecting the fountain to the mains was too high.

One British Rail area manager went on record to explain the shortage of porters at main line stations, saying that they'd become so intimidated by irate passengers that they went into hiding whenever a train pulled in.

QUICK EXIT

There are times when only desperate excuses can save you, when you have to beat a hasty retreat while arousing as little suspicion as possible. These are for emergency use only.

My God, the car's rolling down the drive. The children must have let off the handbrake . . .

A lorry drove through the sitting-room wall in the middle of the night. They're trying to hush it up because it was carrying warheads to Greenham Common but it's knocked us for six . . .

I've been mugged . . .

Oh no! I've just remembered that I haven't told the babysitter that we set the burglar alarm upstairs. If she goes into any of the rooms except the children's we'll have the Flying Squad on the doorstep again.

. . . No, it's all right, thank you. It must have been the gin (or whatever's being drunk) mixing with the anti-adder serum I was given yesterday. I'll be all right in the morning . . . but if you'll excuse me now.

I don't like to make a fuss, but I'm allergic to cats and I just saw yours helping itself to some of the dip. I've got some pills in the car but they knock me out in a quarter of an hour. I hope you'll understand . . .

My . . . had a stroke. They think only the left side's paralyzed.

Something went wrong with the new fire and the whole thing blew up. Only one of the children was hurt.

A gunman jumped into our carriage and pulled the communication cord. The police got him in the end but they're keeping quiet about the affair because they hope to catch the accomplices as well.

My . . died today.

I felt terrible during the night. There was a sort of tightness in my chest. I woke up with a terrible shooting pain in my left arm. My wife just rang for an ambulance.

We were hanging pictures when a nail went right through a cable in the wall. My husband's out cold and I'm waiting for the ambulance. I must keep the line clear, so if you wouldn't mind hanging up.

We're expecting the dog to have her puppies at any moment and I've only just rushed out to get some things from the vet. Excuse me if I dash.

I've just caught sight of my ex-wife! I can't face seeing her at the moment . . . bye!

ROAD SENSE

'God would not have invented the automobile if he had intended me to walk,' wrote J. E. Morpurgo, giving the motorist the ultimate excuse for his car. Most of the time we have to rely on more down to earth excuses to keep us and our cars out of trouble.

A motorist who appeared before magistrates in Malling, Kent, excused the wobbly wheels on his car by saying, 'When I tightened the wheel nuts before, I tightened them too tight, so when I went to tighten them again I thought if I didn't tighten them so tight they wouldn't be too tight, but I must have tightened them too loose.'

Questioned by police as to why his car had no horn, a Humberside motorist explained, 'I never had any reason for a horn. I can always put a duck out of the window and make it quack.'

'You were travelling at forty miles an hour,' said a policeman to a speeding motorist.

'I can't see how,' he was told, 'I haven't been out an hour.'

A policeman who was booked by one of his colleagues while parked in a restricted area, drew on his own powers under the law as a defence of his action. 'I had to attend this court as a witness,' said PC Ray Redditch. 'I knew that twenty minutes is the parking limit without special permission from a uniformed policeman. I was in uniform and there was no other policeman in sight then, so I gave myself permission.'

☆

'I want a chauffeur who can think quickly in an emergency,' a wealthy company director told a prospective employee.

'Then I'm your man, sir. I haven't had an accident yet in which I couldn't come up with a cast-iron excuse in ten seconds.'

☆

An Indiana highway patrol pulled over a motorist driving dangerously slowly down the middle of an interstate highway. Asked to explain himself, the driver replied, 'I was looking for my dentures, which had been thrown out of the window by accident when they became embedded in the wing of a chicken I was chewing.'

☆

A traffic policeman stopped a car in a built-up area and asked the driver, 'What do you mean by driving at fifty miles an hour along here?'

'My brakes aren't too good,' replied the motorist, 'and I was hurrying to get home before I had an accident.'

☆

Divine inspiration aided a north London woman when she appeared before Hendon magistrates to answer a charge of driving unaccompanied and without the necessary 'L' plates. She denied the allegation that she had been driving unaccompanied and said that although her instructor might have been invisible, his presence could not be doubted since he was none other than Jesus Christ. 'The invisible man was driving my car and I know that was Christ who guides me,' she said. 'He was sitting in the car with me and supervising my driving. I am a Christian and I know that I have not done wrong.'

'Going to a fire?' asked a policeman to a speeding driver.

'Not exactly,' he answered, 'just trying to prevent one.'

'Yes? And how did you propose to do that?'

'Well, my boss told me that's what he'd do if I arrived late again, and I was putting my foot down to get to the office on time.'

☆

An American motor cop finally overhauled a speeding motorist after a hard chase and asked, 'Why didn't you pull up when I shouted back there?'

'I thought you just said "Good morning, Senator" ', replied the driver.

'Well, you see, Senator, I wanted to warn you about driving fast through the next town.'

☆

An Oklahoma driver who'd been proceeding down a state highway in an exemplary manner was asked to stop when police became worried about his passenger. The man had a horse sitting on the back seat. 'The poor old thing was looking so bored out there in the country I thought I'd bring him into town,' explained the driver. The police were not impressed and charged him with drunken driving and horse-theft.

☆

Another American motorist, this time in California, explained when he was nabbed after driving through a red light: 'If I make any sudden moves my wife spills her breakfast and that makes her mad,' he told the traffic cop, and sure enough when he looked inside there was the lady polishing off the last of her bacon and eggs.

☆

An American driver returned to his car and found a note tucked under the windscreen-wiper, explaining why the car had acquired a severely damaged wing in the twenty minutes since it had been parked. 'I have just run into your car,' it read. 'People have seen me and are watching me write this. They think I am giving you my name and address. They are wrong.'

When Mr Robert Gregory appeared before magistrates in Stroud, Gloucestershire, charged with driving without due care and attention he had a clear line worked out for his defence. 'My mind was preoccupied by the thought of my grandson who is in hospital with a broken thigh,' he said, 'my brother who is seriously ill in another hospital, my wife, who is caring for my eighty-eight-year-old mother-in-law and my sister, who has collapsed under the strain of looking after her – to say nothing of the stress involved in the reorganizing of local government.'

☆

An Irish policeman, attracted by a battered Mini, moving down a country lane at little better than a brisk walking pace, ordered the driver to stop so that he could examine the vehicle. His suspicions were well founded. All four tyres were bald, the spare was flat, as was the battery, there was no rear-view mirror and only first gear worked in the gearbox. In the course of the examination the exhaust pipe came away in the officer's hand and the engine boiled. The motorist tried to justify his use of the car saying that he had broken his leg while trying to jack up the car and hadn't been able to find anyone else to drive him to hospital.

☆

A former Lord Chief Justice summing up his job, said, 'The greater part of my time is spent on investigating collisions between propelled vehicles, each on its own side of the road, each sounding its horn, and each stationary.'

Many motorists try the same approach with their insurance companies. Here is a selection of excuses sent in as accident statements:

The pedestrian had no idea which direction to go, so I ran over him.

To avoid hitting the bumper of the car in front, I struck the pedestrian.

My car was legally parked as it backed into the other vehicle.

I collided with a stationary truck coming the other way.

In an attempt to kill a fly, I drove into a telegraph pole.

As I approached the intersection, a stop sign suddenly appeared in a place where no stop sign has ever appeared before. I was unable to stop in time to avoid a collision.

Coming home, I drove into the wrong house and collided with a tree I don't have.

An invisible car came out of nowhere, struck my vehicle and vanished.

A pedestrian hit me and went under my car.

I pulled away from the side of the road. Glanced at my mother-in-law and headed over the embankment.

I told the police that I was not injured, but on removing my hat I found that I had a skull fracture.

I had been driving for forty years when I fell asleep at the wheel and had an accident.

I had been shopping for plants all day and was on my way home. As I reached an intersection a hedge sprang up obscuring my vision. I did not see the other car.

The other car collided with mine without giving warning of its intentions.

I was sure the old fellow would never make it to the other side of the road when I struck him.

Top Twenty Excuses to Traffic Police

The accelerator stuck.

I've just had it serviced and I was checking to see if the fault had been corrected.

I thought my window was down but found it was up when I put my hand through it.

They've just done a report which proves this car can't even go over seventy.

I heard something go in the engine. I thought it was one of the mountings. Stopping suddenly could have caused a terrible accident.

I was on my way to see my daughter/wife/mother in hospital.

The speedometer must be faulty. It was showing sixty-five all the way along.

I couldn't see the sign because of that damned great furniture van.

I thought you were after someone else so I speeded up to make room for you to get by.

I only speeded up for a moment to change lanes safely.

I'm afraid the radio was playing and I couldn't hear your siren.

That car in front was roaring away from me and swerving all over the road. Why didn't you nab him?

All the traffic was going down hill at the same pace. Why pick on me?

The light may have been red when I went through but it was still amber when I reached it, and with the other fellow so close to my bumper I had to carry on. If I hadn't he'd have smashed into the back of me.

I know one headlight doesn't work. That's why I was driving so carefully. I can't get it fixed until tomorrow – Monday.

I had no idea I was going that fast. I'm glad you stopped me in time. The truth is I've just come from spending the whole day in court getting a divorce. It's shaken me up a bit. I promise it won't happen again.

I thought that paper bag back there was a dog. I had to swerve in case I hit it. That's when I must have crossed the line.

It's just on its way to the MOT. From what you've said things don't look too good.

If you think my exhaust is noisy what about all these motorbikes roaring around the place?

Isn't that a coincidence? I was just on my way to buy a new set of tyres.

I was just about to reverse and you don't have to wear the belt to do that, do you?

SHOPPERS' PARADISE

Shoplifting, returning goods, explaining poor service or faulty products – finely honed excuses are found on both sides of the commercial fence.

There was a publicity manager for Thorn Lighting, a market leader in lightbulb manufacture, who assured critics, 'You can dismiss from your mind that we are holding back technical developments. As far as we are concerned, there is no consumer demand for a long-life bulb.'

☆

A customer in a hurry for a new passport photograph dashed into a 'While-you-wait' photographers in the West End, had her photograph taken and elected to stay in the shop until it was ready. Much to her disappointment the assistant told her to call back the next day, adding, 'We only take the photograph while you wait.'

☆

A nun detained by store detectives in an Oxford Street shop was found to have two unworn cardigans stuffed into her handbag. She was charged with shoplifting and appeared before the magistrates where she pleaded that her misdemeanour must have been 'the work of the devil'.

☆

The proprietor of the Love Inn, Cambridge, was more than a little taken aback when police arrived one summer morning with a search warrant and started rummaging through his stock in search of obscene material. 'Good

God, there is nothing here,' he told them. 'This is just a little family sex shop.'

☆

The environmental lobby were duly annoyed to see that an exclusive London jewellers were advertising a whale-bone candle-snuffer among their selection of Christmas gifts. One campaigner felt so strongly on the subject that he wrote to complain about what he saw as another example of needless exploitation of an endangered animal. The firm replied, 'Although we understand your concern with the preservation of the whale, the whalebone that we use comes only from dead whales . . .'

☆

From *The Times* Law Reports: 'Their Lordships rejected a submission that they ought to regard the casual presence of a caterpillar in a tin of peas as "an unavoidable consequence of the process of collection or preparation of food" '.

☆

An apparent misunderstanding over the purpose of date stamps on packaged foods was clarified by a spokesman for one of the country's leading cheese packers who defended the practice of scraping the mould off old cheese and offering it for sale. According to the spokesman, the date stamp referred to the life of the wrapper and not the cheese inside.

☆

In the days before cling-film wrapping and grocery counters as hygenic and sterilized as operating theatres, many customers were alarmed by some staffs' careless attitude to food contamination. One lady customer drew an assistant's attention to one of her colleagues, who was happily coughing and sneezing over an exposed keg of butter without even taking the trouble to stifle his outbursts with a handkerchief. 'Oh it isn't butter,' the girl replied, rising to her colleague's defence. 'It's margarine.'

☆

The enterprising owner of a street stall in London offered the otherwise unappealing china figure of a small boy with one arm broken off under the legend, 'The Infant Nelson'.

☆

When self-service petrol pumps made their first appearance they caused a certain amount of confusion among motorists used to an attendant filling their tanks. One attentive customer carefully studied the instructions on a recently installed pump, wrote his name and address on a piece of paper and slipped it into the slot designed to take £1 notes. When he was asked why he had done this he replied, 'It said "Insert a note", so I did.'

☆

Sign in a car dealer's window:
'Cars new and pre-owned.'

☆

A shopper asked for a small packet of washing powder and was surprised to be handed one marked, 'Large'. When she reminded the assistant of her request, she was told, 'That's right, madam. It comes in three sizes: Large, Giant and Super. I gave you the smallest size – Large.'

☆

As she was walking past a souvenir shop in New York a British visitor noticed a sign in the window saying 'English dollars gladly exchanged', which prompted her to nip inside and point out the mistake in the currency. The proprietor thanked her warmly and after she had made a small purchase confided to her that a good twenty per cent of his tourist trade came from British visitors who felt it their duty to correct his mistake.

The rag-trade has special problems of its own, as one buyer for a leading fashion house indicated when she despaired of the shape of many Midlands customers. 'Nobody knows why the Birmingham figure should be so difficult,' she said. 'It may be something to do with new regulations in the factories. Almost all the girls sit down to work nowadays, and that is bound to have awful results in the end.'

☆

As part of its campaign to get a fairer deal for the consumer, *Which?* cited the case of a woman who spent 130 guineas on a dress only to find that it couldn't be washed or drycleaned. When she complained, the manufacturer told her that he never expected his clothes to be worn more than once.

☆

Among the familiar line of advertisements used to draw the public's attention to Smirnoff vodka was one that fell some way short of the mark. 'I thought the Kama Sutra was an Indian restaurant until I discovered Smirnoff'. After a market survey the advertisers withdrew the ad, explaining that 'Sixty per cent of people did think it was an Indian restaurant.'

☆

An elderly Chicago widow, Mrs Maud Prinz, underwent a remarkable change in lifestyle after she got lost in one of the city's large department stores. Claiming she couldn't find her way out, she spent a month living in the building until she was eventually discovered in the bedding department. 'After the first day I asked a detective the way out,' she explained. 'But he told me that I looked like a tramp and if I didn't get out he would arrest me on suspicion. After that I opened an account and lived off the things I bought, eating in the restaurants and taking a bath at night. I had no one to telephone and soon got used to the new routine.'

☆

Faced with her bill for treatment in a private London hospital a patient questioned the anaesthetist's charge which seemed excessive. '£200 just to put me to sleep!' she complained.

'No, it's to be sure that you wake up again,' she was told.

☆

TIED UP TONIGHT

It might have been all right for Oscar Wilde, who once refused an invitation to a *subsequent* engagement, but most of us don't have the courage or the wherewithal to be quite as open when it comes to getting out of unwanted invitations. Here are a few 'alibis' to keep up your sleeve:

We'd love to come but we'll never find a babysitter at this notice.

We've decided to take an early holiday this year to beat the crowds.

With the pay-freeze at the office I'm afraid we've had to blow the whistle on all excess spending.

I know it's still early but I've just had a hot bath and a couple of sleeping pills and I'm already on the way out.

The dishwasher just overflowed and the kitchen's two inches deep in water.

The freezer's on the blink and I was just on the way through the door with a suitcase full of partially thawed ice-cream, 20 pounds of stewed apple and half a pig in search of a new home.

If only it was not going to be during Lent.

Ever since I was told I've got this allergic reaction/
ulcer/diabetes I've had to lay off the booze completely.
Even a sip is fatal. It would be purgatory to come to one
of your fabulous parties and stay on the wagon all evening.

With any luck I'll be on my way to . . . just about then. I
can't say too much about it, but promotion might be in
the air.

What a pity – we've just sent off the cheque for a concert
season that ties us up for six Saturdays in a row. We only
get the full discount if we go to them all.

I'll try and come if it's humanly possible. It all depends on
my mother's condition after her brain scan the day before.

We've been watching every episode of . . . and that's the
night of the last one. I know you'll understand.

We'll be in the middle of redecorating. It may seem like

an odd time but it's the only opportunity we'll have without the dogs (or the children).

I don't usually tell people but, as it's you, I must explain that I'm working as a trainee Samaritan and tonight's the first one on my own. I know you'll understand; but mum's the word.

You know I'd love to come. It just depends on whether they can arrange bail. (You don't have to say whose).

There have been a lot of break-ins round here recently and until the new alarm is rigged up we're scared to leave the house for too long.

I have to be at work at the crack of dawn tomorrow and I wouldn't want to breeze in and out after you had gone to so much trouble.

I promised myself I'd spend a week-end cooking and stocking up the freezer. There must be a hundred pounds' worth of food waiting to be dealt with now and I can't lose a minute.

My boss has just rung and asked us over for a quiet drink. It's the first time he's ever done this. I've no idea what it's all about.

Her mother will be staying with us.

My husband will be away on business all week and we never go anywhere without each other.

UNAVOIDABLE DELAYS

The wonders of modern transport were neatly summed up by one American businessman who ruefully replied to a question about the speed of Concorde, 'The day I can get from Manhattan to Kennedy in the same time as it takes to fly from there to London, I'll be a happy man.' Faced with mounting hostility and resentment from the consumer and hopeless disorganization and bewilderment from within, the field of transport has seen some of the most desperate excuses yet.

While one of the rash of new motorways was still at the planning stage, a spokesman for the Department of the Environment was challenged over apparent delays in the siting of one of the intersections – a decision considered, naturally enough, by many observers to be fundamental. 'Intersection six is still being planned,' replied the spokesman. When asked if he had any idea where it might be situated, he replied, 'We aren't quite sure. I would imagine it will be between intersection five and intersection seven.'

An alarming rise of 14 per cent in deaths and serious injuries on West Country roads some years ago was blamed by Devon and Cornwall police on the slow reactions of elderly pedestrians.

From a letter in the *Sun*:

During the last six months I have knocked over

no fewer than four cyclists. On each occasion the cyclist was entirely to blame. In future I shall let them take the consequences of their own folly, and make no effort to avoid them.

☆

During the peak holiday rush of 1975 a man telephoned a harassed booking clerk at the Pan Am London office with what turned out to be a hoax bomb scare – not that it made any impact on the clerk who, when he heard the message, 'I've got a bomb on this morning's flight to Chicago,' snapped, 'This is passenger reservations, sir. You should call our freight department.'

☆

A passenger wanting to travel from Tottenham Court Road to Hampstead Heath boarded his usual bus in spite of the fact that its destination indicated Oxford Circus. When the conductor came round to collect his fare he pointed out this discrepancy only to be told, 'There's India stamped on the tyres but we're not going to Calcutta.'

☆

From *New Scientist:*

We take some satisfaction in the fact that Lockheed Tristar powered by RB211 engines, with twice the power of those in Boeing 707-type aircraft, generate no greater noise at take-off than that of the population of Greater London shouting together.'

☆

When a Yorkshire bus company applied to run summer tours from West Hartlepool down the coast to Robin Hood's Bay, British Rail didn't take kindly to the idea. There was already a perfectly good train service, they argued. However, the West Hartlepool licensing authority negotiated the dispute with great diplomacy by saying that there would be no objection to the bus company advertising 'mystery tours'. The destination would be Robin Hood's Bay, it was acknowledged, but the public weren't to know this, and on this basis the licence was granted.

A passenger at Charing Cross was dismayed to find that the train he'd been intending to catch had been cancelled. The ticket collector suggested he should catch a later one to which the man replied, 'That's the slow train isn't it?'

'Not slow,' answered the collector, 'just semi-fast.'

Music came to the aid of Lord Harewood when he appeared at Bow Street magistrates' court charged with two motoring offences. In his defence his lordship pleaded (successfully) that he had not been aware of backing into a car parked behind his own since he had been listening to a Mozart wind serenade at the time on the car radio. It was likely, he told the court, that he had mistaken the horn of the damaged car, activated by its burglar alarm, for a sustained tone on the clarinet.

In the happy days before General Amin, when tourists flocked to Uganda's game reserves, one party flying to the Murchison Falls were told by their pilot they were going to have to overshoot the runway on their first approach. When the aircraft was out of danger the pilot came on the intercom to say, 'Sorry about that, ladies and gentlemen, but we can't land at the moment. There's a herd of white rhino on the airstrip.'

Going her rounds of Douglas, the capital of the Isle of Man, a collector of the RNLI approached a visitor for a donation, only to receive the polite refusal, 'I flew over.'

☆

Despite the empty seats and passengers eager to board his bus in the rush hour, a London conductor employed withering logic when he pushed them back and rang the bell saying, 'If there are five empty seats and I say the bus is full, the bus is full.'

☆

An airline passenger fuming in his seat at a delay caused by a minor repair was reminded by the stewardess that such measures had their uses. 'Remember, sir,' she told him, 'better late than dead on time.'

☆

A ticket collector at Dover had got into the habit of saying 'Good night, Jim,' to a regular passenger on the evening train. For four years he exchanged this pleasantry with the man until one night the passenger took a swing at him and put him off work for a fortnight. When the magistrates asked him to account for his action, Mr B. Davidson replied, 'My name's not Jim, it's Bert.'

☆

A bus inspector at Waterloo was asked by a prospective passenger when the next bus was due. 'We don't have a timetable any more,' he was told. 'We only guarantee same day delivery.'

☆

VIRGIN TERRITORY

There are those who still maintain that the best oral contraceptive is talking your way out of it. This isn't as easy as they make out. Boy meets girl. Boy takes girl out for the evening. Boy takes girl back to his flat. Boy makes overtures. Girl wants to say 'no' without being a prude and without making him lose interest. What does she say?
Here are a few excuses:

Him: Gosh, this flat's cold tonight!
Her: Well, mine isn't.

Him: Don't you want to make tonight a memorable experience? Nothing will be different between us tomorrow.
Her: If it's not going to be different tomorrow, let's just let it be the same now.

Him: You've no idea what you're missing.
Her: Yes, that makes two of us. You don't know what you're missing either.

Him: Do you want to watch the sun rise in the morning?
Her: Just the sun.

Him: I think I can really turn you on.
Her: I think the only things that need to be turned on here are the lights.

Him: Why don't you move over here where it's comfortable?
Her: No, thank you. I'm more comfortable being this far away from you.

Him: I'm lonely. Please stay with me tonight. I just want someone to hold.
Her: In that case why don't you buy a teddy-bear?

Him: If you don't stay, you'll never know what you're missing.
Her: Yes, I do. That's why the answer's no.

Him: Come on, you know you want it as much as I do. Stop pretending.
Her: If that's true, you can't be wanting it very much.

Him: There's no reason why we shouldn't do it. Everyone else does.
Her: That's fine. Then you won't have trouble finding someone else.

Him: I think we could make good rhythm.
Her: I'm sorry, but I don't dance.

Him: Come on; it's good exercise.
Her: Thank you, but I played tennis this afternoon.

If your problems start in bed you need a different range of excuses. Overwork, 'first night nerves', discomfort, they're all worth a try when you fail to come up to expectations and let down the side:

I hurt my back lifting the shopping out of the car. You should see the size of those boxes in Sainsbury's.

I'm sorry. I suppose I'm out of practice.

I'm never any good for a week after I run into my ex-husband.

I got it caught up with my zipper, but I didn't think it would make any difference.

I can't get comfortable on these nylon sheets.

Water beds always make me feel seasick.

I shouldn't have had that last pint . . . where's the loo?

It's impossible when we've been arguing. Let's just lie here and talk, shall we?

You should have had a bath.

I have to read something to get me going and all my books are at home.

Now you know why they call me 'Bunny'.

I can only do it properly to the *Bolero*.

I'm sorry, but for a moment you looked just like my sister.

I'm sorry but I'm worried sick by this current deal.

You should have left those raw onions.

Why didn't you wear that nightie I gave you?

I suppose I was too excited.

That game/dance/journey must have taken more out of me than I realized.

I suppose it's shyness but this always happens the first time, especially with someone I really like.

WORKERS' PLAYTIME

While management have come up with some pretty choice excuses for their errors, they've frequently been matched by those from the shop floor and the union conference table. Industrial relations can be a minefield for the unwary but over the years both sides have managed to stumble through, relatively unscathed, thanks to excuses like these . . .

When the employees of a firm of undertakers resorted to strike action to press their pay claim, one of their leaders spoke on Capital Radio to give their side of the dispute. 'It's very unfortunate,' he told the interviewer, 'but we are fighting for a living wage.'

Even the royal estates are not without their grumblings of discontent over workers' rights. A spokesman for the staff at Sandringham corresponded some years ago with the Duke of Edinburgh about the condition of some of the estate workers' houses. When the press got wind of this, however, the man refused to be drawn on the subject of their wages. 'It's considered an honour to work on the royal estate,' he told reporters. 'There people think they will get their reward in heaven.'

Striking London dockers refused to unload a shipment of melons rapidly deteriorating in a ship's hold on the grounds that the melon is not a working man's fruit.

☆

From an incident form filled in by a London Transport bus cleaner: 'As I was cleaning from the top floor all my tickets and rubbish, my box is at the top, my feet catch the box and I nok it down and I fell down with it. When the bottom cum, my box noks down my buket.

I go up from the bottom and my brush is at the top and I step on it and I slip and I throw my box to the bo-tom.

I go down to fetch my box and I step on it and slip again as my other foot goes into the buket which has the water and I fall again with my foot in the buket.

I come out of the buket and I fill it with water I put it on the top stairs and I go down to my box to bring it up and at the top I step over my buket with my foot but it is wet from being in the buket and I fall back down the stairs and I am hurt.

I am going to put water in my buket again wen Mr Chandler say why I am cleaning *his* bus and I hit him with my buket and I am sorry.'

☆

A South Humberside man who said that he was 'transport manager' at Tesco's was asked to elaborate on this important assignment. 'I look after the trollies in the shop,' he said.

☆

Among the protests against the proposed introduction of the tachograph into British lorry cabs was that of the sec-retary of the Transport Workers' Midlands trade group, a Mr Alan Law. 'The tachograph was first introduced by Hitler for the German army,' he argued. 'Employees should be glad to see them go. There's no evidence that they improve the safety aspect. What the Germans say about them is of no interest to us. They lost two world wars.'

☆

A reporter visiting a mill near Bradford noticed that men worked six frames each while the women worked seven for virtually the same wage. When the foreman was asked to explain this he replied, 'Because it's women's work.'

☆

In certain industries some excuses have gone the rounds so often that they've even been codified. The engineering industry is a case in point. For years the following list has been in circulation on both sides of the Atlantic, where its entries have proved a powerful negative argument in almost any circumstance:

We've never done it before

Nobody else has ever done it

It has never been tried before

We tried it before

Another company (person) tried it before

We've been doing it this way for twenty-five years

It won't work in a small company

It won't work in a large company

It won't work in our company

Why change – it's working okay

The boss will never buy it

It needs further investigation

Our competitors are not doing it

It's too much trouble to change

Our company is different

The ad. department says it can't be done

The sales department says it can't be sold

The service department won't like it

The janitor says it can't be done

It can't be done

We don't have the money

We don't have the personnel

We don't have the equipment

The union will scream

It's too visionary

You can't teach an old dog new tricks

It's too radical a change

It's beyond my responsibility

It's not my job

We don't have the time

It will make other procedures obsolete

Customers won't buy it

It's contrary to policy

It will increase overheads

The employees will never buy it

It's not our problem

I don't like it

You're right, but . . .

We're not ready for it

It needs more thought

Management won't accept it

We can't take the chance

We'd lose money on it

It takes too long to pay out

We're doing all right as it is

It needs sleeping on

It won't work in this department

It's impossible

X-PLANATIONS

There are times, and the fewer the better, when our total exposure demands the most ingenious excuses. Whether we find ourselves locked out of a changing-room in the all-together, or have to try and account for a collection of racy magazines discovered by our nearest and dearest the excuses we come up with have far-reaching consequences that can take us to the dock if we're not careful.

One of the highlights at a Virginian carnival held a few years back was a show called 'G-String Revue' which understandably attracted a large audience, among them members of the local police force. The four artistes featured in the performance were later arrested and charged with 'over exposure', an allegation challenged by one of them when she appeared in court. According to a woman police officer, the girl had appeared on stage at one point in the act in a state of total nudity. This was incorrect according to the girl. She had been wearing a G-string, she said, round her ankle.

☆

A CID sergeant who apprehended a naked man on a train asked, 'What's the idea?'

The defendant, a Mr Harker, replied, 'Everybody has his own peculiarities; this is mine.'

He added that he had been travelling naked on British Rail for the past couple of years but didn't think that anyone had noticed.

☆

A Viennese philatelist, Joseph Berkas, was given an absolute discharge by an Austrian court after explaining why he had rushed into the bedroom of his landlady's attractive 21-year-old daughter, torn away the towel with which she was covering herself, and made a close, fingertip examination of her bottom. He said that he had left a valuable foreign stamp soaking in the bath, and it had disappeared.

After ordering a luminous figurine of the Virgin Mary from an Australian supplier, Mrs Ada Denver, an elderly Queensland resident, was staggered to receive a life-size, artificial penis wrapped in a copy of *Sexual Intercourse – The Full Facts*. The marketing manager of the firm responsible was full of apologies when he was told of the mix-up. 'We deal in sex aids and religious trinkets,' he said. 'We are serious people. We apologize. I am the secretary of the local Vegetarians Against the Nazis group.'

☆

Following a tip-off, the Turin vice squad raided one of the city's massage parlours, which offered among its various delights 'overall body massage with opportunities for meditation', and found that all was not as it seemed. Having gained entry by means of the passwords 'Peace and Goodwill', they caught everyone inside completely by surprise, none more so than a naked priest who was discovered 'deep in meditation' with one of the members of the staff. 'I needed this experience to understand the problems of my parishioners,' he told the officers of the law.

☆

Such was the reputation of Uri Geller's metal-bending powers that one Swedish girl who discovered herself in the family way announced that she was going to take him to court. According to Miss Sigrid Hemse, from Gotland, Sweden, she and her fiancé had been making love while watching his mysterious powers at work on television, during which time her contraceptive device bent out of shape.

☆

A striptease artiste who refused to remove her clothes during a cabaret in a swish Kuala Lumpur hotel was sued by the management for breach of contract. In pleading not guilty the young lady told the court that her refusal to undress on the night in question had nothing to do with the act itself. It was the persistent attention of mosquitoes that had persuaded her to remain fully clothed.

☆

A New York trial featuring a naked 27-year-old model, a photographer and a freelance writer ended with a sensational judicial ruling when the defendants were found not guilty of causing a breach of the peace. After hearing evidence from the policeman who had arrested the trio, the judge decided that there was no case to answer. The fact that the model had been standing on the corner of Broadway and Liberty Street without a stitch of clothing while she was photographed was ruled as being insufficient grounds to bring charges.

'Actually the defendants annoyed no one, interfered with no one, obstructed no one, except perhaps the police officer,' the judge said. 'A breach of the peace requires the presence of the public. The public related to people. There weren't any people there.' And on that basis they were allowed to go free.

☆

The Times carried the following interpretation of a bas relief on a recently opened post office: 'The design consists of a male and female nude, recumbent, but with a suggestion that they are floating in water. Thus the main rhythms are not static, but suggest a movement of circulation appropriate to the transactions of the post office.'

☆

The former Leeds Watch Committee was reconvened to study a fan dancer's act at the Leeds Empire to make sure that it was suitable viewing for the city's wider audience. In an effort to sound noncommittal one of the committee members said, 'Leeds people are very broad-minded, but that is a very different matter from tolerating anything really objectionable. I may go to see the performance myself.'

A Southend woman arrested by the town's police for prostitution said in her defence that as she was blind in one eye and suffering from blurred vision in the other she was in no condition to ply for trade. 'I can only see if someone is right on top of me,' she concluded.

☆

A man accused by police of indecently exposing himself to a neighbour in Chorley, Lancashire, told the court, 'I was not standing naked at the window, but merely passing on my way from the bathroom to the bedroom.' He was then asked why his neighbour had seen him peering round the curtains and answered, 'I had been looking for a mouse in the backyard. I had been intending to shoot it.'

The opening of *Oh Calcutta*! caused a stir in Stockholm when at least six members of the audience turned up to the first night stark naked. They seemed very put out when the management ordered them to leave. As one of them said, 'We understood that you had to be in the nude in order to get in.'

Having pleaded 'not guilty' to a charge of indecent exposure, Richard Bullock gave his version of the incident that had landed him in the dock. 'I was brought up in Nigeria,' he began, 'and when the consequences of the drought became obvious I decided to put the national interest first and perform the *n'dula*, a naked rain dance, on the village green. That night the rain began and continued twenty-four hours. I estimate that up to £500,000 worth of crops were saved.' The court took a less sanguine view and fined him £10.

☆

YES, MINISTER

Official explanations from civil servants, Number Ten, and quangos galore successfully manage to paper over most bureaucratic blunders and irregularities. Only occasionally does the truth emerge and even then there's likely to be a cabinet minister or other well-primed spokesman standing by to pour oil on troubled waters.

Taking up the claim by a group of farmers that their land was polluted, the BBC programme *Nationwide* sent a reporter to the scene to meet an inspector from the Department of the Environment. Holding a jar of soil to the inspector's nose the reporter asked whether he couldn't smell petrol. The man from the ministry said he couldn't, though he did acknowledge that he could detect 'an environmental odour associated with petroleum'.

A Coventry second-hand car dealer who invested in a twenty-foot high statue of King Kong and changed his company's name to complement it was told by the Business Names section of the Department of Trade and Industry that trading under the name of The King Kong Kar Kompany contravened regulations as 'it implies Royal patronage'. The car dealer was furious and threatened to take up the matter with Her Majesty herself. 'There was not the slightest risk of confusion,' he declared. 'At the time I had him dressed up as Santa Claus.'

A farmer in north-east Scotland received a letter from the government department controlling agriculture during the war telling him to carry on with his ploughing since records showed that he had not ploughed his allotted quota. The farmer wrote back pointing out that he had lost a number of men to the armed forces and as a consequence had been forced to stop ploughing once the lambing season began. The ministry replied that he should postpone the lambing season for a month.

☆

From a government form sent to employers:

It is regretted that it was not possible to send the enclosed forms to you before the date by which, had you received them, you would be required to forward completed copies to this office.

☆

After it had been decided to turn the Royal Navy's last wartime destroyer into a museum at Southampton, the chairman of the trust set up to administer it, Vice-Admiral Sir Ian McIntoch, ran into trouble with bureaucratic red tape. Because all the guns aboard HMS *Cavalier* were still in working order, the admiral required permission from the Home Office to have the ship towed from Chatham around the coast. This was finally granted by the issuing of a fire-arms certificate.

☆

An American Army press officer in Vietnam answered journalists pestering him for information about recent US action over Cambodia, 'Bombing! Bombing! Bombing! You keep calling it bombing. It wasn't bombing. It was air support.'

☆

In reply to a request for more regular window cleaning the head of a government building was told by an official of the Ministry of Works, 'I am requested to inform you

117

that additional cleaning of windows to the mezzanine and first floors cannot be considered unless there are exceptional circumstances other than the fact that they get dirty.'

☆

When the late Sid Vicious of the Sex Pistols fame was allowed bail while charged with a drugs offence, one of the conditions was that he surrendered his passport to the police. However, it was later reported that this had been returned. The excuse? Mr Vicious said that he would be travelling abroad in the near future.

☆

Peterborough *Daily Telegraph* once reported the following exchange of letters:

From an Army Captain to the Army Paymaster:
     I observe that my promotion to the rank of Captain is shown in orders as taking effect from 19 May 944. I therefore request that my account be credited with £63,875 as representing arrears of pay now due.

From the Army Paymaster to the Captain:
     In reply to your letter, it is pointed out that since the date therein mentioned the Battle of Hastings has been fought, in the course of which a considerable deficiency of bows and arrows was brought to light.
     Since you appear to be the sole survivor of this incident, your liability in respect of this deficiency, the replacement value of which is estimated at £63,875 6s 8d, cannot be questioned. If therefore you will remit the sum of 6s 8d the matter can be dealt with *per contra* and may be considered closed.

☆

One optimistic tax-payer from Worthing wrote to his local Collector of Taxes informing him, 'I am not liable to Inland Revenue as I live on the coast.'

☆

From a circular distributed in a government department thirty odd years ago:

> Memorandum to Chief Examiners. In conformity with a Treasury order which has just been issued, official correspondence should not refer to the 'devaluation of the £'. Some such phrase as 'the change in the dollar rate' should be used instead.

The Inland Revenue received the following letter from an anxious member of the public:

> I cannot meet the full amount as my husband is in hospital. As soon as I can I will send on the remains.

☆

Japanese police guarding the impressive Tokyo building which was the venue for a seven-nation economic gathering a few years ago, prevented journalists from passing without displaying special permits. When the journalists asked where they could obtain these permits, which none of them possessed, they were given the impenetrable answer, 'Inside.'

☆

A dramatic rise in the success rate of a Scotland Yard campaign mounted against pornography traders thirty years ago led to unforeseen problems. So great did the Yard's stockpile of obscene material become that officers had to start searching for new premises in which to store it. It would have been easier to set light to it all, of course. However, the authorities were banned from burning any of the material because a thick pall of smoke would have contravened the regulations concerning the smokeless zone.

☆

A Royal Navy spokesman detailed to explain the procedure for clearing target areas to a group of interested parties told his audience, 'Patrol launches have orders not to order trawlers away from the area. They merely inform skippers that they are in an area where bombing is about to commence. They usually cooperate by moving.'

☆

A regular correspondent with his local Tax Inspector's office rebuked for not making use of the official reference numbers provided for his benefit replied by return of post, 'Dear Old Pals, We've been writing to each other for so long I thought the time had come to get on more intimate terms.'

☆

When a branch of Civil Assistance, a sort of Home Guard for the nuclear age, was opened in Eastbourne, the organizers were careful to keep the names of members a close secret. They were worried that the KGB might try to infiltrate the movement, they announced.

When the *Daily Telegraph* carried an article by its Naval Correspondent on the Royal Navy's new diesel-electric powered submarine there was an uproar in Whitehall. The paper was accused of divulging an official secret and the journalist responsible taken severely to task until he reminded the Ministry of Defence that it had been they who had supplied him with the figures in question. 'That was in metric tonnes which is not secret,' they told him. However, the process of converting these into imperial measurements was considered tantamount to treason.

☆

Justifying the decision to employ a civic butler the Lord Mayor of Birmingham argued, 'At present, if the Lord Mayor wants to give someone a glass of sherry he has to pour it out himself.'

☆

From a reply to a Parliamentary question:

The fact that the Bill did not appear in the Parliamentary time-table for this session did not mean that it had low priority, but merely that the other measures had a higher priority.

☆

Assessing the career of the foreign secretary charged with masterminding the pre-war policy of appeasement, the *Yorkshire Post* carried the observation, 'I suppose that in the course of his long service to this country, Lord Halifax has committed mistakes. The ideal British statesman must commit mistakes.'

☆

Manufacturers of chastity belts, based in Dorset, were astonished to receive the news that their goods were classified as furniture and were therefore liable to purchase tax. They appealed against the decision, arguing that chastity belts were really safety equipment and on that basis were exempt from any tax.

☆

ZYGODACTYLIC

A 'zygodactyl', in case it has slipped your memory, is a bird with toes arranged in pairs, two in front and two at the back. Not that the meaning is of any significance in this case. In fact the less significance the better, because the ultimate excuse open to us all is the incomprehensible one!

There was a civil servant who, when asked to explain his conduct to a Royal Commission, offered this excuse:

> What I have said has demonstrated that it is very difficult to find an answer to that question, but if I were pressed for an answer, I would say that, so far as we can see, taking it rather by and large, taking one time with another, and taking the average of departments, it is possible that there would not be found to be very much in it either way.

Tactics like this have been an inspiration to many.

A couple who answered an advertisement for a second-hand car, agreed to buy it and produced a social security cheque for £400 as payment. When the vendor questioned this he was assured that there would be no problem with it. 'We're supposed to use it to buy furniture,' he was told, 'but everyone else seems to buy cars with the money.'

A New Zealand yachtsman who sailed into port after completing a voyage from Fiji received the customary inspection from the Customs and Excise. During the course of their search the men from the revenue discovered a cockatoo hidden under the skipper's bunk and immediately accused him of trying to smuggle the bird into New Zealand. The sailor rejected this claim, saying that the bird had accidentally flown into his main mast while he was at sea and had fallen stunned to the deck. Why, in that case, asked the customs officers, was there a sizeable box of bird seed also secreted beneath the bunk! The answer to that was just as easy. The captain said that it was not hidden. It was stowed there so that his wife and he could sprinkle it on top of their yoghurt during the voyage.

☆

In 1972 an Oxford man, Mr Terence Dunklin, rampaged through his house tearing fixtures and fittings from the walls, hurling his television and hi fi through his front window, ripping the telephone from its socket, wrenching the bath from its pipes and destroying his bedroom suite. When he had finally been pacified he was asked why he had done it. 'I was shocked by the overcommercialization of Christmas,' he replied.

☆

A Bangor man charged with fraud admitted using the same coin in his gas meter for almost a year but appealed for consideration since, in his own words, he had done it 'on the spur of the moment'.

☆

A lady who caused concern among her village neighbours by running naked around her garden in the middle of the night explained, 'I had an owl tucked under my arm.'

☆

A Birmingham man accused of causing a breach of the peace was asked by local magistrates why he made a habit of dressing in an unconventional way. 'It relaxes me to wear a black bra under a see-through blouse, panty-hose, silver-plated heels and false eyelashes,' he told the court. 'Such things are worn every day by the London hippy jet-set men. I feel I am being discriminated against on grounds of age.' The court was told that the man was over eighty.

A seminar studying various aspects of road safety were treated to this explanation by a psychologist:

The reason why children have more road sense than their parents is that their parents' first-hand conscious intellections have been inherited by them as inconscioused, that is to say, inherited, intellections, converted by a process of inheritance into second-hand intellections.

☆

A Scottish husband who threw his wife over their banister twice in as many minutes told the policeman who arrested him, 'We were never very close.'

☆

Four Cairo policemen gave the following reasons for diverting a funeral cortège they were supposed to be escorting to a cemetery to the city's race-course. They told the official enquiry set up to investigate the incident that they had been persuaded to go to the races by an irresistible power from the deceased. Once there, a similar power impelled them to back horses the deceased would have put his money on had he been alive. Their faith was not in vain. The horses all won.

☆

The final straw that ended Mrs Dorothy Eagle's marriage was her husband's reply to her bellow down in the garden, 'I'm getting a divorce.'
In answer Mr Eagle shouted back, 'If I don't get these tomato plants in soon, they will die.'

☆

Arguing against the ordination of women one curate from a North London parish told his deanery synod, 'If God had meant women to be ordained, I would not have been born a little boy.'

The Times Law Report some years ago carried this singular exchange:

His Lordship: I suppose the word 'Horse' in the rule does not include an aeroplane.

Counsel: No, I think not.

His Lordship: It ought to, it is much the same.

Counsel: I think that it was put in for the relief of the archdeacon.

☆

A man accused of using an offensive weapon in a threatening manner justified carrying the knife on the grounds that he only used it to chip splinters from his artificial leg and occasionally to help his girlfriend cut up parsnips.

☆

After escaping from a state lunatic asylum in Missouri a patient, Mr Theodore Lieberbaum, broke into a fried chicken stand in the town of Little Rock, Arkansas. Psychiatrists who interviewed him after his arrest tried to discover his motives. 'I heard voices telling me that if I did certain things I could marry Diana Ross,' he announced.

☆

A Royal Navy destroyer came across an unknown trawler flying a bizarre assortment of flags and signalled the enquiry, 'What is the significance of that signal you are flying?'

The trawler replied promptly, 'Regret I do not know. Flags smelt of fish.'

☆

'I just did not know what I was doing,' is an excuse frequently heard by those investigating cases of shoplifting, but the police officers interviewing an actress accused of stealing tinned dog meat were treated to more than the customary pleas for clemency when she continued, 'It has been nothing but work, work, work for the last two years. In over 30 sex films I have performed more than 2,000 erotico-gymnastic acts. You can see that I am dazed by it all because the goods for which I forgot to pay were all dog-foods and I poisoned my alsatian Casanova by mistake last week.'

Travelling salesman Barny Wisman pleaded guilty to a charge of speeding through Lechlade, Gloucestershire, in 1974, but felt compelled to tell the court, 'I forgot myself. But at the far end of the town they were screaming for toilet rolls.'

An Essex youth brought relish one afternoon in a very unexpected way to customers of two Colchester cafes. In the first he grabbed a large plastic tomato and squirted its contents over a lady seated next to him. Soon after this he adjourned to the second cafe, where he mounted the serving counter, seized a similar receptacle, this time disguised as a coconut, and repeated his performance, liberally coating a display of cakes and topping off the barman for good measure. Apprehended shortly afterwards in a nearby pub, he said that he had behaved in this way because he wanted 'to read something amusing in the local paper.'